Pacesetter

SENIOR HIGH VOL. 1

Pacesetter

The Complete Youth Ministry Resource

Help!

COPING WITH CRISIS

David C. Cook Publishing Co.

Elgin, Illinois/Weston, Ontario

Senior High PACESETTER

HELP! Coping with Crisis

DAVID C. COOK PUBLISHING CO.
Elgin, Illinois/Weston, Ontario
HELP! Coping with Crisis

Creative Team

Project Editor: Kevin A. Miller
Editors: Anne E. Dinnan; Paul N. Woods
Assistant Editor: Eric Potter
Designer: Jill Novak

Management Team

Topic introduction by Gary W. Downing

We'd like to thank the many encouragers who helped PACESETTER become reality. —The Editors

Published by David C. Cook Publishing Co.
850 North Grove Avenue
Elgin, IL 60120
Cable address: DCCOOK
First printing, 1986
Printed in the United States of America
Library of Congress Catalog Card Number: 85-72933
ISBN: 0-89191-282-7

Cover photo by Bakstad Photographics

Help!

COPING WITH CRISIS

Teenagers have been called a "population at risk." As you read the newspaper or watch television, you can get the impression that all our adolescents are a troubled group. If they aren't confronting drugs, they are wrestling with sex. How can kids live under such pressure? Are all adolescents in agony?

The facts are that many young people *are* under pressure and are threatened by crises they are incapable of handling. Yet we might forget that many more teenagers are leading healthy, normal lives without undue trauma and anxiety. Young people mirror the larger population and are, in John Powell's words, "the megaphone of the human condition."

As caring Christian adult leaders, we must guard against falling prey to two negative approaches to teenagers. We can either feel overwhelmed at the size of the problems and write all kids off in despair, or we can assume almost every kid is smoking dope, messing around sexually, and heading for institutionalization. Neither caricature is helpful; neither squares with a proper understanding of kids' problems.

In reality, the vast majority of teenagers are *not* vandals, promiscuous, or chemically dependent. While young people have to confront difficult choices and cope with a changing world threatened by war, famine, and economic uncertainty, they have access to the same Jesus we look to for hope, courage, and wisdom.

INSIDE ■ THIS ■ VOLUME

HELP!—Coping with Crisis (Volume One in the PACESETTER series) can help you lead your group through the changes and crises they meet day by day.

First, for background on the topic and your own enrichment, we offer "Expert Insights," articles by leaders in youth ministry. For example, how do you minister to a kid in serious crisis? Check out the article by Rich Van Pelt, director of Road Home Ministries in Denver. Veteran youth worker Jay Kesler and counselor/professor Dr. Gary Collins offer additional insights from their experience.

Then, use PACESETTER's practical programming tools:

■ The "Meetings" section gives you five complete meeting plans on crisis-related topics. Reproduce the activity pieces at the back of this book for use with these meetings.

■ Then there's the "More Bright Ideas" section. Here you'll find around 20 activity ideas, many suitable as meetings in themselves. Use them whenever you need them.

■ Need material for an upcoming retreat? You'll find it in "Breakaway": a powerful retreat to help kids beat bad times.

■ Need a meaningful drama for a youth night or service that's almost here? Turn to the "Kids in the Spotlight" section for a moving piece called, "The Glass Box."

■ Finally, to help you build a coherent, supportive group identity, we've included "Nurturing Your Group" by Dr. Gary Downing.

So if you're looking at a blank calendar and wondering what you're going to do with your kids, you've come to the right place. Whether you need one activity or months of programs, PACESETTER is at your service. □

Contents

Contents

A veteran of crisis ministry offers sharp insights into helping kids in crisis.

Ministering to KIDS in Crisis

RICH VAN PELT
Interviewed by Paul N. Woods

How did you get interested in crisis ministry?

When I began doing youth work 16 years ago, it mattered that you were in touch with the latest and greatest games and the best crowdbreakers and skits. Through the years, youth work has evolved to the point where the youth worker in a church situation has to have skills that were not being given when I was in college and seminary.

I realized that in many difficult issues I was involved in—like suicide, substance abuse, sexuality, and the problem of disrupted families—there were things that I didn't have any preparation for. So my own involvement in the area of crisis, quite frankly, was out of need.

How would you define a crisis?

The professional community would say that crisis is "a period of disequilibrium overpowering a person's homeostatic mechanism." *What?!?!* What they're saying is that a crisis is a time when our normal coping ability short-circuits and we lose balance. It's important to understand that *we* do not define what a crisis is. The person in crisis defines the crisis. When a kid breaks up with his girl friend, we look at that situation and typically identify it as puppy love. But we've got to remember that puppy love is very real to puppies! If we simply allow crisis to be what *we* could call crisis, we're going to miss an opportunity to minister in a lot of people's lives.

How do kids usually handle crises?

A lot of things determine how a kid handles a crisis. The primary one is the support system he or she has. We have a new phenomenon around the country that researchers are calling *peer banding.* It used to be that home was a refuge—it was the place where you could get "suited up" to face what was going on out there. For a lot of kids that's not available any longer. As a result they're being almost *thrust* into the peer group for more support than the peer group can really offer them. They're *banding* in peer group units to have their needs met. But their peers just aren't able to meet all those needs.

If a kid doesn't have the kind of support he needs at home or in the church community, any crisis can escalate beyond what it ever had to. If there are caring, positive, supportive adults around to help a kid have perspective, the crisis likely won't be as serious. The church can be a primary support agency in a kid's life.

Do church kids face the same kinds of major crises that other kids face?

The problems we're seeing are not minority problems. The National Center for Health indicates that this year 500,000 kids in the United States are going to attempt suicide. And at least 5,000 that we'll know about will succeed. One in ten girls in America under age 18 is involved right now in an incestuous relationship. Alcoholism is a major health problem among adolescents. We're not talking about kids outside the church family—we're talking about the kids who regularly attend our youth groups. *Our kids* are affected by the family problems, the substance abuse problems, the suicide problems, the problems in sexually acting out. Studies on sexuality among teenagers indicate that church kids come out virtually no different than secular kids.

How should a youth worker respond when there is a crisis in a kid's life or family?

Typically we've responded to kids and families in crisis by giving them a book, a tract, a tape, or something like "Seven Ways to Beat the Blahs and Achieve Spiritual Victory"—instead of having the kind of significant involvement that we can have. We underestimate the incredible value of relationships that we as youth workers have with kids. Professional counselors first have to develop a relationship. We already have that relationship. We've got half the battle already won.

But because we're often inexperienced in helping kids face major crises, we usually respond in one of two ways. One is *avoidance*, the other is *rescuing.*

I encourage youth workers to recognize that faith involves entering into new territory. The Chinese word for crisis has two characters. The first character means *danger,* the second means *opportunity.* We need to see crisis not as an interruption in our ministry with kids, but as an incredible opportunity.

I used to be afraid of the kid saying, "I'm doing drugs," or "I'm thinking of killing myself," or "I got too involved with my girl friend last night." But now I see those times as some of the *best* ministry times with kids.

When kids get injured at an activity, I always am more than eager to be the person to go to the hospital with them. Because the time when kids are in crisis is incredibly valuable ministry time. A lot of the walls come down and we have a real opportunity to have some impact.

The other response we often have is *rescuing*. Because we care so deeply for kids, we're tempted to do everything we can to alleviate their pain and remove them from the crisis situation. And that can do more damage than good.

What practical things can a youth worker do to help kids through such crises?

There are several steps that are very helpful.

First, *accept the reality of their crisis* as they define it. People who are helpful to people in crisis are people who are willing to accept others where they are. Three words are often used to describe people in crisis: helpless, hopeless, and hapless. There is a loss of self-esteem, an inability to think clearly—people are literally immobilized.

Youth workers need to be sensitive. Sometimes kids will tell us what's going on in their lives. But if we're in significant personal relationships with them and we start seeing or hearing of these kinds of conditions—a kid articulating hopelessness, or helplessness—it might be a wonderful opportunity to say, "I'm concerned about some things I see. What's going on in your life?" To be helpful to people in crisis we must meet them where they are.

Second, *provide reassurance.* This is helping people have some perspective. The other night I passed a serious accident that had just happened. A woman and her three children had been driving down the highway, and two young men who were helping a stranded motorist came running across the highway. She hit them and both of them died there on the spot. It was terrible. I couldn't help the men, but I could help the woman who was terrified—who had feelings like she was going to be put in jail. The kinds of normal feelings that we have when we don't understand that we're not responsible. The way I was most helpful to her was by reassuring her and helping her to relax as best as possible, and to have some perspective on what was going on.

One of the greatest gifts that we can give to kids in crisis is a willingness to listen to them.

We may not have the technical skills that are going to be required to help turn around a chemical dependency or help a kid work through some issues that are causing him or her to be suicidal. But we can, because of our existing relationship, provide reassurance that life can and will go on.

Third, *listen.* People in crisis need to talk. Alan Loy McGinnis in his helpful little book, *The Friendship Factor,* calls listening "the language of love." We have a generation of kids who need caring adults who will take the time to listen to them. As youth workers, we need to work overtime on developing an ability to listen. Listening with more than just our ears. Often kids will tell us much more by their eyes, their body language, or their behavior than they'll tell us from their words. One of the greatest gifts that we can give to kids in crisis is a willingness to listen to them.

The fourth step is *processing the situation.* If we're going to be really helpful, we must learn as many details as we can. We want to encourage the kid to share all the relative information. It can help that kid get in touch with not only information, but with feelings. And then we can determine at what level we can be most helpful.

Then, fifth, move to *focusing.* The helplessness people feel often makes it hard to sort out what really is precipitating the present crisis. When a kid moves into crisis, the crisis situation awakens many other unresolved problem areas in his life. If a kid's father dies unexpectedly, or if his parents announce they're going to get divorced, not only does *that* become the crisis, but everything else in his life that is unresolved comes crashing in on him. Like the exam he has to take. Or the payment on his stereo that he doesn't have enough money for. We can help him sort out the problems that he's dealing with and focus on the primary one. And then get him to listen to alternatives and resources. In a very structured way we begin helping him in his helplessness.

Sixth, *develop a plan of action.* At this point we have to ask ourselves, "Am I really able to help this kid? Am I the best person to be involved?" Referral is not a sign of weakness—it's a sign of strength. As youth workers and as pastors we often get caught up in what I would call three narcissistic snares: that we know all, that we love all, and that we feel all. And sometimes we're threatened by admitting that we don't have the resources. But it's not a sign of weakness to refer. My responsibility is to get kids the best help available. And sometimes that means moving them into a professional counseling relationship.

But often, depending on the nature of the crisis, we can be more than adequate for kids and help them develop a plan of action that will make a difference in their lives. Sometimes we have to ask questions like "Does the environment need to be changed? What are the first steps that can be taken?" We identify those steps, and then we establish attainable goals, including some success experiences that kids can have. They need to see some progress.

Seventh, *provide accountability.* There are going to be kids who simply choose crisis as a life-style. I've had them in every youth group I've been involved in. It's their way of getting attention. Negative attention is better than no attention at all. So in providing accountability we've got to determine, "Does this kid really want to get well?" as Jesus asked in John 5:6.

Crisis call lines across the country have learned that with suicidal kids it helps to develop a contract. It sounds silly, because it's not a written contract, but simply something like, "Will you commit to me that in the next 30 days if you think about killing yourself, before you do anything you'll give me a call and give me an opportunity for the two of us talk?" What that's doing is giving the kid some accountability. It's a tie to another warm body who cares. And it's proven to work. A lot of kids are alive today because of a simple thing like contracting.

The last thing is to understand that healing takes time. Psychologists suggest that it often takes kids as much as two years to work through the kind of grief that's associated with something like losing a parent or divorce. And we think that if we meet with a kid for a couple sessions he should be well: "Next, please." We've got to recognize that we're working with people. And healing often takes time.

Give us an example of a time this has really worked.

I spoke at a camp recently and saw that one young lady was really struggling through some stuff, but she wasn't talking about it. I showed her I could be her friend, got to know her, and by the end of the week learned that this year she—a Christian kid—had gotten involved in casual sexual escapades, which resulted in a pregnancy which was terminated in abortion. And the kid felt like garbage. This gal was really suicidal and said so. As a result of spending time with her, I believe that she really has moved into a new dimension of her living experience. It's going to take some time, but God's in the process of freeing her from that sin, and helping her to move on in her life. If I had simply avoided that situation I would have missed a wonderful ministry opportunity. And perhaps by my avoidance have missed a great opportunity to affect her life.

As youth workers our primary responsibility is to help kids become independently dependent on Jesus.

Any other tips for youth workers ministering to kids in crisis?

I just want to underscore that we can't overestimate the value of relationships with kids. Even in referral it's critical that I maintain my relationship with the kids. I've moved them into a professional relationship with a doctor who may help them, but I'm the one who's going to have the continuing relationship with them, not that doctor. Youth workers *can* make a difference. Crisis is one of the greatest gifts that we have in our ministry with kids—the opportunity to offer the grace of God and the love of God and the forgiveness of God and the comfort of God. II Corinthians 1 talks about "the God of all comfort." We might freely translate the Greek of this expression, "the God of all coming alongside." In crisis we can allow "the God of all coming alongside" to come alongside those who hurt and who need the presence of Jesus—by coming alongside them ourselves.

Finally, we need to recognize that we can't do all that we want to do. Kids are going to come to us with needs and problems that far outweigh our knowledge and our experience. But it's important to remember that we can provide a caring relationship that gives kids emotional strength as they face tough times—and at the same time, point them to a relationship with Jesus Christ. As youth workers our primary responsibility is to help kids become independently dependent on

Jesus. We're more than social workers. We're more than counselors. And part of our responsibility is learning the skills we need to be helpful when kids need us. □

Recommended Resources

The Friendship Factor, Alan Loy McGinnis, Augsburg Publishing House

How to Be a People Helper, Gary Collins, Vision House

Real Friends, Barbara Varenhorst, Harper and Row

The Young People's Yellow Pages: A National Sourcebook for Youth, Alvin Rosenbaum, Perigee Books

The Question, Fred Carpenter, director, Mars Hill Productions

Rich Van Pelt *is a chaplain with the Colorado Department of Corrections—Division of Youth Services, and director of Road Home Ministries in Denver, Colorado. He is involved in the Family Research Council of America in Washington, D.C., and leads seminars for Youth Specialties.*

Paul Woods *is editor of youth publications for David C. Cook Publishing Co.*

Crisis Counseling

What to do when a kid wants you to promise not to tell anyone his problem

We need to be very careful in making that kind of commitment. There are times when other people have to be involved. If a kid tells me that she's involved in an incestuous relationship, or if a kid tells me that he's going to kill himself, I have a moral responsibility to preserve life, not friendship. And I'd rather not be in the bind of having made a commitment to tell no one and then have to violate the commitment.

In my own ministry with kids, I've come to a point where I will never say yes to that kind of a request. I say, "You've got to trust my commitment to you that I'm going to handle the information you give me in your best interest." I think that's a lot more honest. I've done this for years now, and I've never had a kid say, "Well, then, I'm not going to talk to you." What kids need is the assurance that we're not going to tell the world.

Rich Van Pelt

□

Which Adults Do Kids Turn To?

Surprising results for youth workers

In a recent survey of high school juniors the question was asked, "What adult would you choose to associate with if you wanted to enjoy the company of that adult, seek guidance from that adult, or gather information from that adult?" Parents were the adults most frequently chosen. I was delighted that ministers and youth ministers were the most frequently mentioned nonrelated adults. Youth workers have been working to develop that kind of credibility among kids and their families for years. Now we've got it.

Rich Van Pelt

Eating Disorders

Increasing number of young women victimized

She wakes up in the morning terrified she is going to spend the day alternately stuffing herself with enormous quantities of food, then compensating by forced vomiting or overdoses of laxatives. She promises herself that she will stop the habit, only to eat a box of crackers, a family-size bag of doughnuts, five Pop-tarts, and 15 Ex-Lax. She has done this three or four times a week for the past five years. Although she is viewed as attractive, intelligent and talented, she feels inadequate and deceitful.

She is one of a growing number of young women affected by bulimia.

Bulimia, bulimarexia, or *binge-purge syndrome* is a serious and spreading eating disorder especially among young women, typically teenagers or women in their twenties. Bulimics are generally older and more self-assured than anorexics. Significantly, anorexics often do not realize that they are sick. Bulimics invariably do. Both, however, typically come from middle-class, upwardly mobile families; they are usually success oriented and viewed as "good children."

Because bulimics tend to secretly binge and purge, and because the syndrome occurs at *all* weights, it is relatively difficult to spot. However, if an outgoing, good student becomes withdrawn, if she demonstrates recurrent weight fluctuations, if she exhibits increased dental problems, and if the glands around the face and neck swell (an effect of frequent vomiting), she may be bulimic.

The possible effects of this syndrome are serious and can be fatal.

Adapted by permission from Marianne Szegedy-Maszak, SUCCESS WITH YOUTH REPORT (Pace Publications)

Reactions to Divorce

Here's a list of reactions you may expect from young people who are experiencing a family divorce:

1. discipline problems
2. dependence
3. rebellion
4. depression
5. grief
6. loss of self-confidence
7. insecure feelings
8. inability to concentrate
9. self-image problems
10. loneliness
11. anger
12. fear
13. emotional detachment
14. anxiety
15. inability to trust anyone
16. cynical attitude
17. close attachment to friends
18. shame, embarrassment.

Adapted by permission from Gary Richardson, GROUP Magazine

Help for Pregnant Teens

■ *The Evangelical Child and Family Agency* (1530 N. Main, Wheaton, IL 60187, 312-653-6400) can refer you to services nationwide for pregnant teenagers. ECFA also provides an adoption service.

■ The directory for the *National Association of Christians in Social Work* (Box 90, St. Davids, PA 19087) lists Christian counselors in every part of the United States.

■ For help and information on alternatives to abortion in your area contact *Bethany Hotline* (1-800-BETHANY), 901 Eastern Ave., NE, Grand Rapids, MI 49503.

Adapted by permission from CAMPUS LIFE Leader's Guide.

Expert Insights

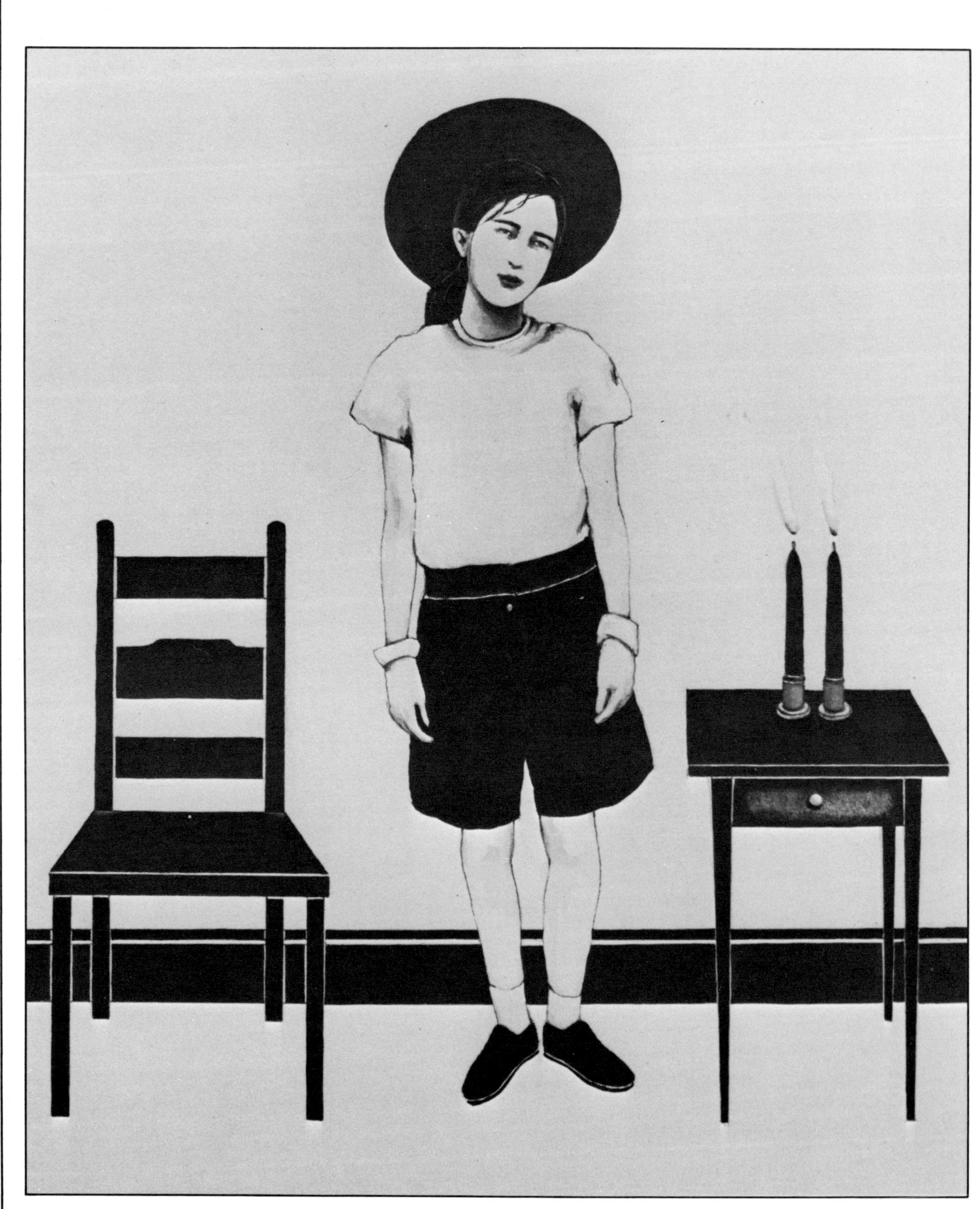

Illustration by Dagmar Frinta

TROUBLE on the Home Front

Helping kids with crises at home

Lauri tried to convince herself that she was worrying over nothing. She didn't dare to think how her parents might react, and she was afraid to share her worries even with her closest friend. When she could bear the tension no longer, Lauri finally mustered the courage to confide in the school nurse. Sure, she knew about teenage pregnancies. Like most kids today she had friends who had gotten pregnant. But Lauri had never dreamed it would happen to her. Like many others in the same predicament, Lauri struggled with guilt and confusion. She was scared to tell her boyfriend, and even more afraid to tell her parents.

BY GARY R. COLLINS

She wondered how the kids at school or in her youth group would react, and suddenly she was faced with questions that never had concerned her much before. Is it okay to have an abortion? Would she have to drop out of school? Should she get married—at age 16? If she decided to have the baby and not marry, should she keep it or put it up for adoption? If she kept the child, would her mother have to raise it?

At times we all face crises, but often they hit teenagers with greater force. High school kids have little experience in coping with stress, their perspectives are narrow, and often they have neither the wisdom nor the power to take action when a crisis strikes. Sometimes kids struggle alone, but often their crises are like Lauri's. They become publicly known, overwhelming, fear inducing, and incapacitating. Often the crises are closely tied to the lives of other people, including one's family and sometimes the leader of the church youth group.

Two Kinds of Crisis

There are two types of crisis: the unexpected and the ongoing. Newspapers report on *unexpected* crises every day: the gang member being shot, the father being killed in an accident, the family losing all its possessions in a fire, the child being kidnapped. Each of these throws a family into sudden crisis. Unexpected discoveries can be equally traumatic: a kid's mother having cancer, the family having to move, one's girl friend being pregnant.

Then there are *ongoing* crises. These are always present, weighing on the minds of family members and creating both anguish and tension. Constant bickering in the home is an example, and so is the persisting alcoholism of a family member or the severe shortage of money that some families face almost constantly.

Knights in Shining Armor?

How do we help teenagers in the midst of such crises? I suspect most of us would like to be rescuers. Like a knight in shining armor who snatches a young damsel from the evil clutches of some horrible dragon, we would like to pull kids out of their painful situations and help them avoid the entangling pressures of life.

But that, of course, is almost never possible. Instead, the sensitive youth worker has the challenge of helping young people face and cope with the crises of their teenage years. In doing this, several guidelines can be kept in mind.

> ***Like snatching a young damsel from a dragon, we would like to pull kids out of their painful situations.***

First, make contact. This seems almost too simple to mention, but few of us like to face other people's crises, especially if we are not invited to be involved. It is easier to get on with our work and hope either that the crisis will resolve itself or that somebody else will handle the situation.

When I am tempted to avoid painful situations, I try to think of Jesus with those two men on the road to Emmaus (Luke 24). They were confused and struggling, in the midst of a spiritual and intellectual crisis, but Jesus didn't wait for them to make an appointment for counseling. Instead, He went to walk with them while they struggled. In a crisis, your mere presence can often be a comfort and a source of help.

Next, try to reduce anxiety. Model calmness in your words and actions. Encourage the teenager to talk, especially about his or her fears and worries. Some people need to hear that it is okay to cry or to express feelings of despair, frustration, or anger. It helps to realize that sometimes the anger may seem unjustified, and it might even be directed against you, in spite of your efforts to help.

At such times you can continue to offer acceptance and encouragement, but try to be realistic. Don't promise that a dying family member will be healed, for example. You don't know that. But you do know, and can say with confidence, that God cares and is in control.

Then you can help the young person evaluate his or her resources. Are there other people in the family, church, or community who could give practical help? Does the teenager have some skills or strengths that could be useful? Is he or she willing to draw on the power of prayer and be aware that God gives special grace to help in times of need?

Keeping the Crisis in Focus

In crisis counseling, it usually is best to focus attention on specific issues. Lauri, for example, needed help in deciding who to tell and how she should break the news to others. She needed to know what to do in terms of school and prenatal care. She needed help to answer her disturbing questions about abortion, marriage, guilt, child care, and "Why did it happen to me?" She also needed time to get things in perspective without being pushed to make quick decisions. In a crisis, some things need to be decided quickly, but other issues can wait.

In the midst of crises, people often are easily influenced by suggestion. Many are inclined to uncritically accept the advice of others. Be careful, therefore, in making suggestions. Try to focus on one issue at a time and, whenever possible, involve the crisis victim in the decision making.

As a crisis counselor, you are likely to feel that you don't have all the answers, but you may know of others who can give guidance. Even your reassuring presence can do much to help the teenager and his or her family as they decide what to do next.

The Greatest of These Is Love

In all of this try to instill hope. Pray for the people in need, asking God to bring comfort and wisdom. Gently share from the Word of God and try to present a realistic perspective, especially when the teenager or the family slips into self-defeating thinking.

When I was in graduate school, I once took a course in crisis counseling. One day the professor made a very simple statement that I have never forgotten. "When you counsel someone in a crisis," he said, "Rule Number One is to let them know that you care and are available." If they can also see that God cares and is available, He may often work through you to bring healing and help to people like Lauri—in the midst of crisis. □

Jesus didn't wait for the two men on the road to Emmaus to make an appointment for counseling.

Dr. Gary Collins *is professor of psychology at Trinity Evangelical Divinity School, Deerfield, Illinois. He has written numerous books and articles on human relationships, including* One to One: How to Help a Friend, *a Christian Growth Elective for high school juniors and seniors (David C. Cook).*

Help! I Can't Handle It!

When to refer a person in crisis to someone else.

Every crisis counselor faces situations that are beyond him or her. These are the times to bring in the experts. When should you refer someone to a professional counselor?

Consider referring when the teenager appears to be:

- deeply depressed or severely disturbed
- suicidal
- extremely aggressive
- controlled by drugs or alcohol
- irrational
- in need of medical or legal advice.

Remember that every community has experienced pastoral counselors, professional therapists, doctors, social service agencies, legal aid societies, police departments, and school guidance counselors or teachers who can give practical guidance whenever you feel stuck.

Calling on these people does not mean that you have failed. Sometimes a referral can be the best help you can give to a teenager in a crisis.

Dr. Gary Collins

The Everyday CRISIS

BY JAY KESLER
with Kevin Miller

How to help kids with the normal ups and downs of adolescence.

Adolescence is an uneven time when the juices and secretions come at irregular rates and create mood swings, confusion, and difficulty. No one understands these changes altogether.

Suppose you notice that a kid is having a terrible time. If you ask him what is wrong, he'll probably say, "Oh, nothing." Most of the time, it isn't anything you—or he—can put a finger on. It's everything from growing up, to feeling unsure about his physical self, to feeling unsure about his future, to feeling unsure about his acceptance with others.

Youth workers sometimes miss these everyday adolescent struggles because they think, "That's normal; he'll grow out of it." Or, "Boy, do I remember those feelings. I'm glad that will pass." The young person, however, may feel overwhelmed by such a "small, normal struggle."

Two Crisis Factors

Young people encounter two factors that make something a genuine crisis for them—even though that same situation would probably not be a crisis for an older person.

First, young people, because they are young, lack a sense of proportion. To a 15- or 17-year-old, anything that happens seems huge. It sits against a very short span of life, so it's a large part of what is him or her. Later, when the young person has more life to put it against, the same situation doesn't seem so big.

Take, for example, a major crisis such as divorce and remarriage. The typical mother who is divorced remarries in 3½ years. A relatively short time in her life, this may encompass all a young person's teenage years. Thus, something often becomes a crisis because the young person doesn't have enough life behind him to put the situation in perspective.

Second, part of maturity is the ability to find alternatives, to work out creative solutions. Kids tend to paint themselves into a corner. They don't see that there are various ways of approaching a situation.

If a grenade were to come through the window, kids would

think: "I can either let it blow up me and everybody else, or I can throw my body on top of it and save everyone." They don't stop to think, "Maybe I can throw it back through the window." Young people tend not to see these options—which is itself a definition of adolescence or immaturity.

Practical Principle #1

The first principle I follow in helping kids is: "Always take kids seriously." Property is an extension of a person, so if you violate the person's property, you do something to violate him. In the same way, if you violate a kid's problem, you violate him. When youth workers downplay a kid's problem, or don't take it seriously, they downplay the kid himself, because the problem is attached to the kid. The most damaging thing a youth worker can do to a young person is not to lack answers (all of us lack answers), but put down the kid's problem, and thus, his life.

If you downplay a kid's problem, you downplay the kid himself.

Once a woman said to me, "My husband has made my life totally meaningless. He has crossed out my life. I try to talk to him about things that take up my life—the broken screen door, the drippy faucet, the car that won't run. He says, 'I don't have time for that,' or 'Get someone else to do that.' He's forgotten that these things are the stuff that makes up my life. Because he refuses to discuss these things with me, he has really destroyed my life."

When a leader refuses to take a kid's problem seriously, the young person will find someone else to listen. A junior high girl may be a little chatterbox that drives people crazy. But if you don't give her enough time, she'll find someone, with less noble motives than yours, who *will* give her time. I think this is why many junior high girls get pregnant. They're looking for someone to give them time and attention.

Most high schools gear themselves to the typical kid. Across the street from the school, you'll find kids whose needs and problems don't fit into the acceptable center range. These kids find each other and become very close. There is an unwritten loyalty among kids who are in these negative peer groups. Unfortunately, these groups reinforce the negative prejudices kids have brought: "My parents don't understand," or "Teachers pick on me," or "They don't understand my hurts." Trivializing a kid's problem forces him closer to a group like this.

Practical Principle #2

Many kids think, "I will never grow out of this problem. This will never pass." They need help to see that people do survive problems like theirs.

So share from your own experience, if you've experienced the same sort of thing. Don't say, "My experience and yours are exactly the same," or "I understand what you're going through." But try to get close enough to the young person's struggle to identify with it.

When I think of my youth, one of the greatest sources of growth in my life was certain men who

I want to honestly share my real struggles and feelings with youth.

allowed me to see their weaknesses and struggles even though I was half their age. When I was about 19, for example, my dad actually told me about a big struggle of his and allowed me to draw my own conclusions. I will never forget that. I now consciously try to give that same sense of worth I felt to young people I meet. I want to level with youth and honestly share my real struggles and feelings with them. Once in a great while I feel exposed or even betrayed by this. But the rewards far outweigh the risks.

So a leader needs to be vulnerable enough to confess his foibles and faults to a kid, rather than always tell how he overcame. He needs to admit he also faltered at these areas and still turned out okay. That assurance is very, very important to young people.

□

Jay Kesler *is president of Taylor University, Upland, Indiana. He has worked with youth for over 30 years, much of that time as president of Youth for Christ. Among his books relating to youth is the landmark* Parents and Teenagers *(Victor).*
Kevin Miller *is editor of ministry resources for David C. Cook Publishing Co.*

Meeting A

It's a Rough Life

Aim

To encourage kids to persevere through life's difficulties, relying on the comfort and presence of God. Key passage: John 16:33.

Overview

Crisis and conflict are inevitable parts of growing up. In fact, it is through conflict that we grow. This session will help teens accept the fact that they will experience some pain in growing up. But beyond that, it will give them hope because of God's presence with them now and His plans for their future.

You'll Need

1. It's a Rough Life (Checklist) 10-15 min.
   - ☐ Crisis Checklist (activity piece A1 from the back of this book)
   - ☐ pencils
2. The Quick Fix (Skits) 15-20 min.
3. Bubble Busting (Bible study) 15-20 min.
   - ☐ balloons or light, plastic, food storage bags
   - ☐ pin
   - ☐ slips of paper
   - ☐ Bibles
   - ☐ Sentence Starters (activity piece A2)
   - ☐ pencils
4. Hang in There! (Prayer) 5 min.

BY ANNE DINNAN

Meeting A

1. It's a Rough Life

(Checklist of crises) 10-15 min.

Discovering that problems are a normal part of everybody's life. Get kids moving and thinking about the normal crises of life with this warm-up activity. Hand out pencils and copies of the "Crisis Checklist" (activity piece A1 from the back of this book). Tell kids to go through the list and check any of the crises they have experienced. Then have them mill around the room to find at least one other person who has experienced each crisis they've checked. When they find someone, they should initial each others' lists.

Call time in about five minutes and find out how many checks most kids have, how many initials they were able to get, and which crises were most common.

Jot the one biggest problem you're facing right now on the back of this paper.

■ Think silently: How are you feeling about this problem or situation right now?

I'm glad you came tonight. If you've got problems—and we just saw that everyone does—then this meeting is for you. We're going to face our problems and get God's help to handle them.

2. The Quick Fix

(Skits) 15-20 min.

Making skits to spoof advertisements that offer instant solutions to life's problems. Advertisers offer a quick fix to any problem. They just never seem to consider the fact that you might have a more serious problem than bad breath or dandruff!

Have students come up with advertisements that offer instant solutions to *real* problems. For instance, a spray that prevents bad relationships. Kids can really ham these up. The point is to satirize the idea that life's problems have instant solutions. Give them about ten minutes to brainstorm ideas in groups of three or four, then come together to perform their impromptu skits.

Discuss what makes these ads unrealistic.

■ What makes us expect our problems to be solved so easily?

Point out that several factors may influence our expectations. One is technology. We grow up expecting machines to do our dirty work.

In medicine, even if we can't cure the disease, we can take some mood-altering or pain-masking drug so that we won't really care.

The problems on TV shows get solved within 30 or 60 minutes, with time out for commercial breaks. Even some Christians in the media preach that if Christians have enough faith they'll always be prosperous and happy.

As you discovered from the checklist we did, real life isn't like that. It's difficult. Sometimes we think we're the only people going through problems, but as you saw, everybody has problems and they don't go away with a spray of deodorant or a swish of mouthwash.

■ **Does this encourage you or depress you? Why?**

Scott Peck, a psychologist, has written a book called *The Road Less Traveled.* The opening sentence is, "Life is difficult." His point is that people would be a lot healthier emotionally if they'd just come to terms with that fact.

■ **Do you think that's true? Why or why not?**

■ **How can it help you to have the perspective that life is going to be difficult rather than a perspective that expects things to always go well?**

Move on to the Bible study to see what Scripture has to say about what to expect from life and how to find real help in crisis.

---

3. Bubble Busting

(Bible study) 15-20 min.

Personalizing God's promises regarding suffering. Before the meeting, copy the following passages of Scripture on slips of paper and stuff each one in a balloon: Genesis 3:19; John 16:33; and James 1:2-4.

Divide kids into three groups; be sure each group has Bibles and paper and pencil. Give each group one of the balloons you prepared. Tell them, "If you expect life to be a bowl of cherries, I hate to burst your bubble, but . . ." Then have each group pop its balloon and study the passage inside to answer these three questions:

■ **What does this passage say about what to expect life to be like? Why?**

■ **Where does suffering come from according to this passage?**

■ **What promise does it offer (if any)?**

Here are some observations your kids might come up with:

Genesis 3:19 tells us to expect life to be very hard. It describes how Adam's sin in the Garden of Eden brought a curse upon mankind. Sickness, frustrating work, and ultimately death are a result of that sin. (It isn't just Adam's sin that causes suffering in the world. If you want to delve into the topic of the consequences of our personal sin, have kids compare and contrast Exodus 20:5 and Ezekiel 18:20.)

In John 16:33, Jesus clearly tells His disciples what to expect from life. As Christians, we sometimes suffer misunderstanding and persecution from the non-Christian world. We are also called on sometimes to sacrifice our personal wishes and well-being for God's work. That means life may not be as easy or seem as pleasurable for us as for others. But Jesus declares His supremacy over the evil in the world and promises us His peace which is far more lasting and satisfying than temporary pleasures the world may offer.

James 1:2-4 explains that suffering has a purpose for the Christian. Suffering is to test our faith. It helps us grow and strengthens us—*if we let it!* The end result of enduring trials is that we will be mature, or complete.

Help kids personalize these truths by filling in the "Sentence Starters" (activity piece A2).

4. Hang In There!

(Prayer) 5 min.

Discussing specific problems kids face and encouraging them to rely on God to help them through. Discuss the "Sentence Starters" you just did and let kids talk about specific problems they are facing right now. Don't force anyone to share aloud. Give them the option to think silently about these questions, or to write down their feelings.

■ **Has our meeting tonight helped you view your situation differently? How?**

■ **What difference, if any, does it make to be a Christian as you face this situation?**

This is still a good question to ask even if not all your kids are Christians. Be ready to share how being a Christian has helped you cope with the difficulties you've faced in life.

Close your meeting with prayer thanking God for His presence and peace. Pray that He will give your group strength to endure their problems.

Make yourself available to kids after the meeting and encourage them to talk to you personally about any problems they are facing. □

Anne Dinnan *is editor of youth publications for David C. Cook Publishing Co. She has contributed to the award-winning* Young Teen Action *series (Cook), and works with teenagers each week at her church in Elgin, Illinois.*

□

Meeting B

Coping With Tough Times

Aim

To provide kids with a strategy for coping with crisis. Key passage: Proverbs 15:21, 22.

Overview

Everyone experiences tough times. Kids, especially, can be overwhelmed by their problems. They need a specific and simple strategy for coping with complex problems.

You'll Need

1. Tied in Knots (Game) 5 min.
2. Wheel of Awareness (Problem identification tool) 15-20 min.
   - □ chalkboard and chalk, or newsprint and markers
   - □ Awareness Wheel (activity piece B1 from the back of this book)
   - □ pencils
3. Peter's Tangle (Bible study) 10-15 min.
   - □ Bibles
   - □ pencils
4. What's Tangling You? (Personal-crisis inventory) 10-15 min.
   - □ Personal Inventory (activity piece B2)
   - □ pencils
5. Taking First Steps (Sharing and prayer) 5 min.

BY MARK WICKSTROM

Meeting B

1. Tied In Knots

(Game) 5 min.

P*laying a game where kids must untangle themselves from a human knot to learn about problem solving.* Start your meeting by having kids form a big clump in the middle of the room. The more participants you have, the better. You will need at least five or six. When everyone has formed a rather tight clump, have everyone grab two hands—not from the same person. Then, *without letting go* of each other, kids must untangle themselves to form a circle. It *can* be done!

■ **How did you manage to untangle yourselves?**

Explain how crises are similar to being tangled up in a knot like this. We need to carefully look at our situations, figure out what steps to take, and move one step at a time, or else we'll be overwhelmed. The key passage for this meeting is Proverbs 15:21, 22. Read it together. Explain that you're going to look at some expert wisdom on how to get untangled from problems.

2. Wheel of Awareness

(Self-examination tool) 15-20 min.

L*earning a technique for solving personal problems.* Brainstorm some typical problems kids encounter. Write these on a chalkboard or sheet of newsprint. Then hand out copies of the "Awareness Wheel" (activity piece B1 from the back of this book) and explain it to kids. *(The Awareness Wheel is trademarked and was developed by Interpersonal Communications Programs, Inc., 715 Florida, Suite 209, Minneapolis, MN 55426. Authors Sherod Miller, Elam Nunnally, Daniel Wackman. Adapted by permission from* Talking Together.*)*

At the center of the wheel is an *issue*. This is anything that needs to be resolved. It can be something as insignificant as what I should wear today, to something as significant as who I should marry.

Around every issue are five spokes. Each of these areas has an impact on an issue.

The first is *sensory data:* What you see, touch, taste, smell, or hear about an issue.

Next are *thoughts* about the issue. Thoughts are based on your interpretation of the sensory data.

Third, are *feelings*. These are affected by your thoughts. You probably have positive feelings (happy, excited, expectant) about good thoughts, but negative feelings (anger, hurt, anxiety) about bad thoughts.

The fourth spoke is *intentions*. What would you like to do about this issue or situation? These are the options or alternatives available to you.

The last spoke on the Awareness Wheel is *action:* what you actually choose to do about an issue.

If my *issue* happened to be what to eat for lunch, I might *hear* my stomach growl and *see* my watch hands strike noon (Sense).

I *decide* I'm hungry and I'd like a burger (Thought).

I might then get *excited* and *anxious* to eat (Feel).

I *think* about getting a burger and walk to my car (Intend).

I then *drive* to Burger World, *order* a burger, and *eat* the burger (Action).

■ **How can knowing your feelings, thoughts, and so on, about a problem help you cope with it?**

Kids should see that breaking a problem down in this way can help you separate conflicting emotions and work through to the heart of the matter.

Have kids form pairs to practice using the Awareness Wheel on some of the problems on the board. When you think they understand how it works, move to the Bible study for another experience in using this tool.

---

3. Peter's Tangle

(Bible study)
10-15 min.

Studying the Bible using the "Awareness Wheel." Have kids read Mark 14:66-72, about Peter's tough time after Jesus is arrested. Then use the "Awareness Wheel" to study the passage:

■ **What is the issue Peter faces?**

(If recognized as Jesus' follower, he may be jailed.)

■ **What sensory data does Peter experience?**

■ **What thoughts might Peter have?**

(Aware that people recognize him. Knows he's outnumbered. Concerned about what people might do to him if they know he's with Jesus.)

■ **What *feelings* might Peter experience?**

■ **What *intentions* might Peter have?**

(At first to protect himself: Be quiet, unnoticed. Next, to defend his lies. Finally, to cope with the pain of failing his Friend, Jesus.)

■ **What *actions* does Peter take?**

■ **Now that we've taken apart Peter's problem, can you identify where he went wrong?**

Obviously, his actions were wrong, but kids should probably see that his thoughts and intentions were also off base. He was legitimately concerned about himself, but he allowed his fears to overshadow his concern for Jesus. He didn't think through the consequences of his actions, and so he failed the Lord.

Peter's failing was very human and Jesus forgave him (John 21:15-19). His experience is only an example to show how dissecting a crisis can help us figure out what actions we can take.

---

4. What's Tangling You?

(Personal-crisis inventory) 10-15 min.

Examining personal problems and identifying steps to deal with them. Hand each kid a copy of the "Personal Inventory" (activity piece B2). Give them five to ten minutes to fill it out. All response sheets should be anonymous with only sex and grade as distinguishing information. (Collect these at the end of the meeting.)

Encourage kids to use the Awareness Wheel to identify how they might work on their personal answers to Question #5. They can use the back of their "Awareness Wheel" sheets for this.

■ **Once you have used the Awareness Wheel on your problem, try to identify one step that you can take to solve it.**

---

5. Taking First Steps

(Sharing and prayer) 5 min.

Sharing action steps with partners and praying for each other. The passage you read at the beginning of this meeting talked about the importance of counsel and advice. The Awareness Wheel is one piece of sound advice, but kids also need personal advice and prayer. Assign each kid a partner. Give partners the last five minutes to share as much about their problems as they feel comfortable sharing and then pray for each other. If they want to show partners their Inventory sheet, they may.

Collect the "Personal Inventory" sheets and stress that you are open to talking to anyone who needs you. You might also encourage students to seek the person mentioned in Question #8.

After the meeting, read over the sheets to alert yourself to any severe problems that exist, and use these sheets in your personal prayer for your group.

Mark Wickstrom, *a pastor at St. Andrews Lutheran Church, Mahtomedi, Minnesota, has nearly 20 years of youth ministry under his belt—as high school teacher, street minister, Young Life leader, youth minister, church consultant, and seminary instructor in youth ministry.*

□

Meeting C

Suicide Is Painful

Aim

To inform kids of the facts about suicide and to allay their own possible fears. Key passage: Luke 15:1-33.

Overview

A myth develops when people feel powerless to deal with something they don't understand. When it comes to suicide, myths abound. If there's anything we feel powerless about, it's teen suicide. In this meeting, you can begin to tear down the myths surrounding suicide and give kids some power to cope with their own fears, as well as to help friends and loved ones.

You'll Need

1. Feeling Sculptures (Awareness activity) 5 min.
2. Myth or Fact? (Quiz) 5-10 min.
   - □ pencils and paper
   - □ Myth vs. Fact (activity piece C1 from the back of this book)
3. Lost and Found (Dramatic Bible study) 15-20 min.
   - □ Bibles
   - □ pencils and paper
   - □ Lost and Found questionnaire (activity piece C2)
4. Dead-End Journey (Intervention roleplays) 15-20 min.
   - □ chalkboard and chalk, or newsprint and markers
5. Group Contract (Commitment and prayer) 5 min.

BY MARK WICKSTROM

Meeting C

1. Feeling Sculptures

(Awareness activity) 5 min.

Identifying with the feelings that lead some people to commit suicide. Introduce the subject of suicide by having kids perform impromptu freeze sculptures. Hand out slips of paper with a feeling written on each: *empty, friendless, depressed, lonely, worthless, hopeless,* etc. Kids try to depict that feeling using only facial expression and body position. As each kid performs his or her sculpture, have the others guess what feeling is being conveyed.

Explain that we all have these feelings, but sometimes they can lead to suicide. Suicide is the second largest cause of death among 12- to 25-year-olds.

Suicide is a frightening topic. We're going to try to find some answers and some help in this meeting.

2. Myth Or Fact?

(Quiz) 5-10 min.

Taking a quiz to determine myth from fact regarding suicide. Lay the factual groundwork for this meeting by giving kids a quiz. Hand out paper and pencils. Read each of the myths on the Myth vs. Fact sheet (activity piece C1), and have kids answer true or false to each one. When each student has responded to all eight myths, hand out and discuss copies of the Myth vs. Fact sheet.

All answers to the quiz are false. Emphasize that jokes or talk about suicide are *never* to be taken lightly.

We've seen that we all have feelings like loneliness, depression, and fear. Sometimes these feelings can lead to suicide. We need to understand that God really cares about us.

3. Lost And Found

(Dramatic Bible study) 15-20 min.

Performing a dramatic Bible study to show how much God values every human being. Form three small groups and assign each one of these parables: Luke 15:1-7, 8-10, and 11-33. Have each group read its parable and plan a short dramatic presentation based on it.

After the groups have performed their dramas, ask:

- **What do these parables reveal about God?**
- **What can we learn about people from these parables? What is God's attitude toward us?**

(Everyone has value and is worth saving. God loves everyone.)

Pass out copies of the Lost-and-Found questionnaire (activity sheet C2) and have kids complete them privately. (If short on time, have kids do them at home.)

4. Dead-End Journey

(Intervention roleplays) 15-20 min.

Roleplaying possible intervention strategies for people considering suicide. Now that you have discovered some facts about suicide and felt God's reassurance of each individual's worth through the Bible study, you are ready to talk about some intervention strategies. The following *Levels of Suicide Experience*[1] will help students understand that any talk about suicide is a sign of a person on a journey that could very well end in self-destruction. Write these six levels on a chalkboard and discuss examples of each.

Level 1: SUICIDE IDEA—The thought of suicide crosses the person's mind.

Level 2: "JUST TALK"—Casual expression and jokes about death or suicide. Idea entertained frequently.

Level 3: GESTURES—A *planned* action that is *low risk,* but meant to make an *impact.* Who will notice?

Level 4: THREAT—A sincere sharing or announcement of intending to die. Again, who will notice?

Level 5: ATTEMPT—Definite risk; a strong, last, desperate warning.

Level 6: COMPLETED SUICIDE—Death occurs.

Have students in small groups roleplay some responses to a person at each level. To help kids prepare, ask:

- **What does a person at this stage need?**
- **What could someone say or do to help?**

Some insights[2] to debrief the roleplays:

Level 1—Thought: What's wrong with me that I'm so down? Why am I the *only* one depressed? Insight: *Everyone* feels depressed at some time or another. What's important is how we deal with it.

Level 2—Thought: Everything's going wrong; no one loves me; no one cares what happens to me. I might as well be dead! Insight: Kids who feel depressed have feelings of emptiness, "nonperson" feelings.

Level 3—Thought: Why doesn't my depression go away? Why doesn't anyone notice I'm hurting and help me? Insight: When kids feel depressed it's hard to see past their own emptiness. It's a very self-centered stage.

Level 4—Thought: I don't want to bother other people with my problems. They don't want to listen to them anyway. Why bother? I'm just a burden. . . . Insight: When teens feel alone, they often think people don't care—they become more isolated and depressed.

Level 5—Thought: Will anyone even notice if I die? Will anyone care? Insight: It is critical to let teens know they are valuable, worth listening to, and important to us. They need to be told they are important to God, too.

Obviously, kids won't become experts on suicide intervention in one meeting. Stress that the best intervention a friend can offer is to refer a suicidal friend to others for help.

If you have a suicidal friend, GET HELP! Do not keep it to yourself thinking you are doing your friend a favor. If you suspect that a friend is suicidal, ask. And if you're right, tell someone—your pastor, a teacher, or a counselor.

---

5. Group Contract

(Commitment and prayer) 5 min.

Covenanting to support each other. One effective method of intervention that professional counselors have found is the *contract.* A counselor will often ask a suicidal person to contract not to act until they have talked together (see Rich Van Pelt's article, "Ministering to Kids in Crisis," earlier in this book). If your group is close, make a similar contract.

1. Anyone in the group considering suicide must not act without first telling someone else in the group his or her intentions. 2. Anyone in the group who knows someone who is suicidal must tell a group leader.

Close your meeting with a group prayer. Make yourself available to talk to kids. □

Footnotes and Sources

[1]Dr. Susan Erbach, Director of Minneapolis Children's Medical Center. Excerpts from a speech given at St. Thomas College, St. Paul, MN.

[2]Instructor insights based on materials by Dr. Irene Jozzelyn, Psychologist

John Janeway Conger, *Adolescence and Youth.*

Mark Wickstrom, *a pastor at St. Andrews Lutheran Church, Mahtomedi, Minnesota, has nearly 20 years of youth ministry under his belt—as high school teacher, street minister, Young Life leader, youth minister, church consultant, and seminary instructor in youth ministry.*

□

The Best Worst Thing That Ever Happened to Me

Aim

To help kids view their problems as opportunities for growth. Key passage: Hebrews 12:1-16.

Overview

Problems, conflicts, crises—nobody wants them, yet inevitably they push their way into our lives, bringing pain and, if we let them, growth. This session will help teens accept the fact that bad times can contribute to their continuing maturity. Beyond that, it will encourage them to trust God to bring good from even the worst situations.

You'll Need

1. Tough Stuff (Case studies) 10-15 min.
   - □ Tough Stuff Cards (activity piece D1 from the back of this book)
2. Actors Anonymous (Skits) 15-25 min.
   - □ Cue Cards (activity piece D2)
   - □ chalkboard and chalk, or newsprint and markers
3. The Truth Test (Bible study) 15 min.
   - □ Bibles
4. Gloom to Growth (Prayer) 5 min.

BY LUCY F. TOWNSEND

Meeting D

1. Tough Stuff

(Case Studies) 10-15 min.

Rating the severity of problems. Before the meeting, copy and cut apart three or four sets of the "Tough Stuff Cards" (activity piece D1). When kids arrive, have them form three or four groups (three or more kids each). Each group should choose a contestant for the "Tough Stuff Matching Game." Contestants should leave the room while each group rates the situations on all six of the "Tough Stuff Cards."

When the groups have rated all the case studies, bring in the contestants. Read aloud each case study in turn and have contestants try to guess how their team rated each one. Teams should then hold up their cards to show their actual choices. Each match is worth 100 points. The team with the most matches is the winner.

■ **Think silently; don't answer. What is one problem you're facing right now?**

Emphasize the idea that we all face problems. What counts is how we respond to problems. The rest of the meeting will help them discover good ways to respond to the problems they're facing.

---

2. Actors Anonymous

(Skits) 15-25 min.

Acting out some ways people respond to problems. In advance, copy and cut apart the "Cue Cards" (activity piece D2). Explain that groups will now have the chance to compete in an acting contest. They will hear about a problem situation. Each group's challenge is to put on a skit showing one way that a youth group might respond to the problem. Read aloud the following:

Last week, your youth group made chocolate chip cookies for the people in a nearby nursing home. This week your youth group leader reads a letter from the people in the nursing home. They loved the cookies and look forward to your next visit. Then comes the bad news. A messenger from the trustees arrives and informs you that he has received many complaints about the kitchen. You often leave it messy, and last Sunday it was in horrible shape. How might your youth group respond to this criticism?

Arrange your kids into five groups and supply each group with a "Cue Card." Allow them to practice several minutes, then have them present their skits.

Ask kids to sum up the strategy each group used to cope with the problem. List these on a chalkboard or piece of newsprint:

- Ignored the problem
- Placed all blame on others
- Attacked the people who criticized them
- Felt sorry for themselves
- Ran from the problem

■ **Think about these strategies. How well would they help solve bigger problems, like the ones we read earlier? How well would they help you solve the problem you're facing right now?**

Explain that there are a lot of different ways we can respond to problems in our lives. The Bible gives us some solid strategies for handling tough situations.

---

3. The Truth Test

(Bible study)
15 min.

Learning Biblical strategies for dealing with problems. Explain that back in the first century, Christians were often beaten, imprisoned, and killed for worshiping Christ. Hebrews 12 was written to encourage them in their suffering. It contains helpful advice for anyone coping with hard times.

Keep the same groups as before and have them come up with a list of Biblical strategies for coping with hard times based on Hebrews 12:1-16. Use the following discussion questions to help them understand the passage.

■ **What does the writer compare the Christian life to? What does it require?**

■ **What effect does sin have as we run this race called the Christian life?**

■ **What benefit does this "cloud of witnesses," and Jesus' own suffering, have for us?**

■ **In verses 5-7, how should we look at hard times?**

(As God's training. God disciplines all Christians. If you are not disciplined by God, you are not "true sons.")

■ **Why does God discipline us?**

■ **Does every Christian learn as much as he or she can from a tough situation?**

(Not necessarily. Christians who "have been trained by" discipline become more righteous and peaceful. This verse implies that some Christians do not learn from their hard knocks. Those who are willing to learn will mature.)

■ **(See verses 14-16) What specific things can we do or not do to grow mature as Christians?**

The previous verses indicated that the goal of God's discipline is our increased holiness. These verses explain specific ways to live godly lives.

When kids have discussed the passage and come up with their list of Biblical strategies, write their answers next to the negative coping strategies you listed in Activity 2.

Answers may include:
- Don't get discouraged and give up your faith.
- Follow the example of Christ and hang in there.
- Accept hard times as discipline from God.
- Get rid of a sin that is keeping you from growing.
- Try to learn as much as you can from the situation.
- Remember that God loves you and wants to help you.

Point out that most of these important coping strategies involve attitudes. If you believe that God is going to bring good from a tough situation, you'll still be in pain, but it won't be unbearable. But if you become bitter, your suffering will be compounded by all the problems bitterness brings.

---

4. Gloom To Growth

(Prayer) 5 min.

Praying about good ways to handle tough situations. Have kids look at the negative coping strategies of the five youth groups (Activity 2). Then have them look at the Biblical coping strategies (Activity 3).

- **Think about the biggest problem you are facing right now. Don't answer out loud. Which of these approaches comes closest to the way you are handling it?**
- **Which approach comes closest to how you would like to handle it?**
- **Is your own sin part of the problem? If so, what can you do about it?**

To bring all these principles down to reality, share some experience of your own in which a difficult time turned out to be a positive experience. Let kids share any times like these that they've experienced as well.

Close your meeting with prayer, asking God to help kids respond to their crises in Biblical ways, and comfort them in painful moments.

Dr. Lucy F. Townsend *is a free-lance writer from Elgin, Illinois. Lucy speaks and writes frequently about Christian education. She has contributed four courses to the award-winning* Young Teen Action *series (Cook).*

□

Meeting E

How to Help a Friend

Aim

To help kids gain skills in helping their friends who are experiencing crises. Key passage: II Corinthians 1:3-5.

Overview

Often kids can help other kids in crisis better than professional counselors can. An existing relationship of trust and care can be the perfect start for helping someone going through a major time of difficulty in his or her life. By learning a few skills, kids really can help their friends.

You'll Need

1. Never Happen to Me? (Crisis examination) 5 min.

   □ In the Next Thirty Minutes (activity piece E1 from the back of this book)

2. Who Cares? (M*A*S*H* discussion) 15-20 min.

   □ chalkboard and chalk, or newsprint and markers

3. Coming Alongsiders (Bible study) 10-15 min.

   □ Bibles

4. Giving a Hand (Crisis helper guidelines) 15-20 min.

   □ Crisis Helper Guidelines (activity piece E2)

BY RICH VAN PELT
with Paul N. Woods

Meeting E

1. Never Happen To Me?

(Crisis examination) 5 min.

Seeing that many friends will probably experience crises within their high school years. Begin by asking the following question:

■ **If we had an absolutely terrible meeting tonight, and everything went wrong, how many bad things could possibly happen in the next 30 minutes?**

After kids have had a chance to respond, hand out copies of "In the Next Thirty Minutes" (activity piece E1 from the back of this book), and go over the statistics there. Then go over the list again and have kids raise hands or stand up if they know someone who is experiencing, or has experienced, each crisis.

Major crises are not a minority problem. These statistics indicate that at least one of these major crises will affect every one of you in some way during your high school years. You will know, or possibly know now, someone who is experiencing a major crisis. And you may be able to be a big help to a friend in need.

---

2. Who Cares?

(M*A*S*H* discussion) 15-20 min.

*Discovering and discussing the ways people either helped or hindered in crises on the television show, M*A*S*H*.* Ask your kids how many of them watch *M*A*S*H** on television. Reruns are watched by a majority of kids around the country.

Why is this show so popular after it's been out of production for several years? Most likely because there's a sense of community. The people shown have joined together around a task, even to the point of bleeding for each other. They are friends to friends in crisis. The relationship you have with a person matters as much in a crisis as the skills you have for counseling.

Write the following headings in a chart on a chalkboard or sheet of newsprint: "Effective Crisis Helper" and "Ineffective Crisis Helper." Have your kids think of a character from *M*A*S*H** and tell why that person is effective or ineffective as a crisis helper. Fill in the chart as kids give you their suggestions. Below are some answers your kids might give. If kids don't come up with many names, suggest some of the names below and let them decide who was effective, who wasn't, and why.

EFFECTIVE CRISIS HELPER

Radar: always there
Klinger: efficient
Hawkeye: able to make you laugh
Potter: experienced, supportive

Hot Lips: take-charge person
Mulcahey: compassionate
Sidney: approachable, good listener
Henry: humorous

INEFFECTIVE CRISIS HELPER
Charles: no sensitivity
Hot Lips: too pushy, stiff
Frank: no compassion
Flagg: general jerk

If Sidney was mentioned late or not at all, you might point out that he was the professional—the one who was *supposed* to help people in crisis. But most of the others were thought of first.

Discuss the insights your kids brought up. Ask how particular traits help people in times of crisis. Have kids come up with a portrait of a good crisis helper.

---

3. Coming Alongsiders

(Bible study) 10-15 min.

Seeing from Scripture how God intends for us to help others in need. Explain to kids that God has something to say about crisis helpers and have them open their Bibles to II Corinthians 1:3-5. Read the verses aloud as your kids follow along.

■ **What word keeps coming up again and again?**

In the NIV, the word *comfort* appears five times. Discuss what this word means, encourage kids for their good responses, and then discuss the questions below.

The words translated "The God of all comfort" could almost literally be rendered "The God of all coming alongside." It's the same root word as the one used to speak of the Holy Spirit as "The Comforter."

■ **What do you think Paul is saying by calling God "the God of all coming alongside"?**

■ **Why did Jesus "come alongside" us by coming to earth?**

■ **How can we "come alongside" others in need?**

Wrap up this discussion by having your kids summarize what this passage is saying to us.

Exploring practical guidelines for helping friends in crisis. Divide your kids into groups of four or five and hand out copies of "Crisis Helper Guidelines" (activity piece E2). Then have kids go over the sheet in their groups. Have each person in the group share one of the principles he or she wants to work on in a relationship with a friend.

If you want to provide extra food for thought, paraphrase the following story for your kids:

Erma Bombeck had been through a hard week. By the time she got to the airport, she was ready to be alone, relax, and read, while she waited to board the plane. As she settled into her book, she heard an elderly woman next to her say, "I'll bet it's cold in Chicago." Without smiling, Erma returned flat, clipped responses to what the woman said. Nevertheless, the woman continued talking, soon unfolding that she was taking her husband's body to Chicago to be buried. After 43 years of marriage, he had suddenly died. With a start, Erma's heart woke up. She realized another human being was screaming to be heard, and in desperation had turned to any stranger. This woman wasn't asking for advice, information, or even consolation. She wanted a living person just to be willing to be present while she talked. The woman talked numbly and steadily until it was time to board the plane. Then she moved on to find her seat in another section. As Erma hung up her coat, she heard the woman's plaintive voice say to her new seat companion, "I'll bet it's cold in Chicago." Erma prayed, "Please, God, let her listen."

Close your meeting by encouraging kids to be sensitive to hurting kids around them and to put into action the skills they have learned in this meeting.

Rich Van Pelt *is an author, speaker, and youth worker from Denver, Colorado. He has experience as a chaplain with the Colorado Department of Corrections—Division of Youth Services and has been involved in the Family Research Council of America.*

Paul Woods *is editor of youth publications for David C. Cook Publishing Co.*

□

4. Giving A Hand

(Crisis helper guidelines) 15-20 min.

More Bright Ideas

1

Humpty-Dumpty

Everyone knows the tragic story of Humpty-Dumpty. His short "life" can be an excellent illustration of how we feel when faced with a crisis. To get into this illustration, choose three or four competitors and give each one a set of repair materials (glue, tape, rubber bands, etc.). Next, bring out eggs (it would be best if the contents of each egg had been previously removed) and drop them off a "wall" into separate containers. The idea is for each contestant to put his/her egg back together again.

2

Job Study

Probably no one has ever experienced more crises than Job. Use the Book of Job as a supplement or do a study of its message. An excellent resource is the Christian Growth Elective course, "Why Me, Lord?" featuring seven inductive studies of the Book of Job. Ask about the types of crises faced by Job, how he responded, how the friends responded, and how they should have responded, and how God fit into the whole picture.

Moving Movie

Show the Mel White movie, *Though I Walk Through the Valley*, the true story of a man dying of cancer. He and his family "play" themselves and are interviewed about their feelings, etc. The film is available through Gospel Films (1-800-253-0413). It is an excellent discussion starter.

BY DAVID VEERMAN

4

Picture a Feeling

Go through magazines and newspapers and cut out pictures that evoke specific emotions or portray someone in the midst of crisis (e.g., someone crying, a person in a hospital bed, the moving van backed up to a house, a boss wearing a frown, etc.). Hold up the pictures, one at a time, and ask kids what they think the person is going through, what he/she is feeling, what would help most in that situation, etc.

More Bright Ideas

5

Group Support

Using the entire group, see how many ways kids can work together to support as many people as possible. These may include building a pyramid, joining hands as a base and letting others lie on top of them, standing and leaning on each other, etc. It is important that everyone is involved and that *they* think of the ways. Discuss how else they can "support" each other, besides physically, and when support might be needed.

6

Draw A Crisis

Write out a number of crisis situations and put them in a box. At the meeting, use small groups and have each draw a crisis and discuss how it would respond in a similar situation. After a few minutes, have the groups report to the whole group. Discuss their crises and responses.

7

First Aid

Break into groups and give them the assignment of assembling a "first-aid kit" for crisis victims. They should use their imaginations and include everything that they feel would be absolutely necessary and most helpful. Have the groups report what they included in the kits and discuss.

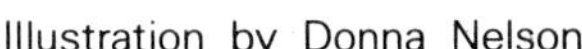

Illustration by Donna Nelson

8

Pocket Survival

List a number of crises on the board including divorce, breaking up with a boyfriend/girlfriend, moving to a new town, natural disaster, severe illness, etc. Have everyone take out his or her wallet/purse and look for resources or symbols of resources which would help them cope. (Examples: money?, pictures of friends or family?, car keys?, report card?, Bible verse?, etc.) Discuss the viability of each potential resource.

9

Book Study

Use the book, *Where Is God When It Hurts*, by Philip Yancey (Zondervan/Campus Life) or *Joni*, by Joni Eareckson (Zondervan), as a supplemental resource or as a discussion starter.

Breaking Point

This game takes advance preparation, but begins a meeting and provides a strong visual demonstration of what happens "under pressure." Gather an assortment of balloons of varying shapes and colors. Decide beforehand how many people you want in a group (e.g., pairs, threes, fours, etc.) and have the balloons grouped in those numbers *according to shape*. In other words, if you decide on "fours," in one pile of balloons you would have four long, thin ones (with a variety of colors). Once these balloons have been chosen and sorted, mix them up again and bring them to the meeting (deflated, or course). As kids enter the room, give each one a balloon and tell them to hold the balloons until further notice. Then, at your signal, they are to inflate their balloons, tie them off, find the other people with the same-shaped balloon, and, in a group sit down on the balloons to burst them.

11

Looking For Help

Bring one (or more if possible) concordance and look up all the verses listed under the word *help*. After each verse is read, decide if it offers help in times of crisis. Make a list of these verses and choose a few to memorize.

12

Good News, Bad News

Do this with individuals, pairs, or teams. Give each one a piece of paper and pencil and have kids write their own "good news and bad news" jokes. Collect jokes and read them. Discuss real-life "good news and bad news" situations.

13

Windfalls & Bankrupt

Using index cards or pieces of paper, make your own "money" by writing a value on one side of each. Divide the cards equally in values from 1 to 10; make enough so that each person will have five. Shuffle and distribute the cards. Explain that for a few minutes everyone will mill around the room, trading cards, but these will be "blind" trades. That is, no one will be able to see what he or she has drawn from others' hands until after the cards are in his or her own hands. A person must always trade when asked, but he or she may bargain about how many cards to trade at a time. A person may not make two trades in succession with the same individual. The object of the game is to have as much money as possible when the game ends. Afterwards, discuss the experience, asking how kids felt about losing high-value cards, how they felt when all they had were low-value cards to trade, how they felt when they drew a windfall, how they felt having the lowest total, etc.

14

Moving On

This is a race to highlight one aspect of what it is like to move. Many families are quite transient and so quite a few kids should be able to identify with this process. Use three or four competitors and give each one a folded-up box, tape (to use in forming the box), and a pile of items which must be packed. These items should be of a variety of shapes and sizes. See who can get the most items into his or her box within a couple of minutes.

15

Current Crises

This activity may be done as a contest between kids or an exercise for the whole group. Distribute a number of newspapers and have kids circle (or tear out) as many crises as they can find. Every section of the newspaper is fair game—front page, sports, editorial, classified, comics, etc. Discuss the types of crises, why they considered them crises, how they were resolved, etc.

Hangman In Crisis

Do a "crisis" version of the old game of hangman. That's where someone thinks of a word and puts blanks (------) on the blackboard for the number of letters in the word, beneath a picture of a gallows with noose. The other person guesses letters which may be in the word. For each right guess, the letter is written in the appropriate blank. For each wrong guess, a part of the hangman's victim is drawn. The goal is to guess the whole word before the victim is hung.

Play the game in teams. Before the meeting, write a dozen possible words or phrases from which the teams must choose: *divorce, funeral, daily stress, devastated, bankrupt, hurricane,* etc. Use these phrases to lead into discussions on crisis.

17

Ups & Downs

Take the whole group to a children's playground and play on the swings, teeter-totters, slides, etc. (Be careful not to displace any children or to break anything.) Besides being a lot of fun and a good break in the usual meeting format, the games are all very illustrative of the "ups and downs" of life. Later, during your discussion, have individuals or small groups design illustrations or talks using the games as object lessons.

18

Emotions Duel

Do this as a champion vs. challenger game. Begin with two contestants, and name an emotion that they are to exhibit with all their might. Let the crowd choose the most expressive person and crown him or her as champion. Choose a challenger and repeat the contest with another emotion. Continue until you tire or run out of emotions. Possible emotions: hatred, fear, love, joy, sadness, happiness, grief, etc. Discuss how each of these emotions comes into play during crises in our lives.

19

Through It All

Bring an inner tube and see how fast you can get the entire group through it. If you have a large crowd, do this as a team event. Have a practice round and then an official one. Later, discuss what made it difficult or easy to get through the tube (e.g., someone pulling or pushing, verbal encouragement, knowing that everyone else had to go through it, too, etc.). Then ask how this experience parallels "going through" crises and difficult situations. Finally, discuss the words to the song by Andrae Crouch, "Through It All." Close by singing it together.

Dave Veerman, *national Campus Life consultant for Youth for Christ, has spent more than 20 years in youth ministry. He contributes regularly to* Campus Life Leader's Guide, Moody Monthly, *and* Group, *and has written several books.*

20

Obstacle Course

This activity will work best in a gym or outdoors. Divide into teams and take representatives from each team out of sight. Next, arrange an obstacle course using chairs, boxes, natural boundaries and foliage, etc. Bring back the blindfolded representatives and place them at the starting line. Explain that they are to walk through the course as quickly as possible with the first one through declared the winner. They will find their way by listening to the shouted instructions from their teammates, a few feet away. (You may want to add time for every obstacle bumped.)

Initiating a GROUP

A critical time for any group is its beginning. Here's how to avoid pitfalls as you shape a new group.

BY GARY W. DOWNING

It all began with a phone call. The scheduled driver was sick, and they wanted me to drive a bus for a retreat. I said yes. Six months later they put me in charge of the group. *Now* what was I supposed to do?

At the time I just waded in where angels fear to tread. I didn't know enough to raise some basic questions, like "What makes a group effective?" I relied on my instincts, a little prayer, and my previous experience to guide me. I figured that since I had been a part of many groups growing up, I would just do the same thing over again. However, I forgot that most of the groups in which I had shared had been sometimes boring, unproductive, and not personally affirming. I didn't understand basic principles for effective group work.

What Makes a Group?

Psychologists tell us whenever two or three people gather together, you have a group. Whether you gather as a "societal cluster" around a common interest, or because of a common need, or because of elements like age, vocation, or status, you have a "group." However, most groups are not initiated with an eye to structures that help support a successful experience.

For example, maybe you have been given charge of a tenth-grade Sunday school class. You discover when you try to plan a social event that you have teenagers from three different high schools. Though you are talking about unity on Sunday mornings, on Friday nights their athletic teams are trying to kill each other.

Putting people who happen to be the same age in a room does not necessarily create a real group. Instead of glossing over the internal differences in a clustering of kids, acknowledge them and work towards overcoming those separating factors over time.

What Makes a Group Leader?

Just because you happen to be older and designated the "leader" by some person or committee, does not necessarily mean you are the authentic leader in your group. There are formal, positional leaders who carry the title. There are also informal, relational leaders who carry the real clout in a group. Leadership has to be earned and learned in a group setting.

The different personalities in a group and the history and purpose of the group call for different styles of leadership. Some groups need direction and limits and, therefore, a more authoritarian leader. Other groups will become withdrawn and dysfunctional under authoritarian leadership because they need someone to come not as the authority, but as a facilitator for the group process. And, some groups seem to operate well without any one identified leader. To come to a group in the wrong way will result in difficulties that need not happen. Be aware of the needs of a group, its expectations and dreams, as well as your own strengths, weaknesses, and primary personal style.

What Makes a Group Effective?

Youth groups today may well be different than the groups in which we participated as youth, because today's adolescents, in many ways, are different. To give just one example, today's teenagers watch well over 15,000 hours of television by the time they graduate from high school. This calls for faster moving, more visual methods to be employed in communicating with them.

Having said this, however, I want to hasten to add that leading a group is *not* impossible.The main thing you have to give as a Christian adult is your own *life.* Your caring relationships with teenagers are the best basis for leadership. Let God's Spirit use your life to lead some younger folk who need your loving leadership.

Activities to Help a New Group

1. When you go to a coffee party or a neighborhood social function, how do you go about meeting someone new? If you're like most people, you catch someone's eye and simply say "hi." After the initial contact you most likely start asking questions to find out what the two of you have in common.

You can follow the same process in your new group. Use openers like "What's your name and how did you get it?" or, "Tell us your name and one fact about yourself a lot of people might not know."

What you are doing is beginning a process of history sharing that happens almost anytime strangers meet. We start to get to know other people by sharing simple facts about ourselves that help them begin to feel more comfortable around us.

Some history-sharing openers to use:

- The nicest thing ever done for me was . . .
- My favorite toy when I was a child was . . .
- My best friend in grade school was . . .
- My most enjoyable holiday is . . .
- My most embarrassing moment I can share was . . .

2. If the first stage in developing relationships in a group is for members to share things they have in common, a second stage is to have people offer particular distinctions which can be affirmed. People are not all the same. It is important in the process of initiating a group to look for ways to build self-esteem and warmth between the participants through personal affirmation. I enjoy talking about my life if I feel people are listening and that they care. I like to listen to other people share if they are being open, honest, and genuine. Again, getting each member to share around some "affirmation questions" is a way to create an environment of warmth and safety people seek in a group. Some to try:

- My favorite sport (or song, musical group, TV show, movie) is . . .
- My greatest hope in life is . . .
- I feel best when I am . . .
- My greatest hero (fictional or real) is . . .
- One thing I like about me is . . .
- One positive change I would like to make in the world is . . .

□

Dr. Gary W. Downing *is executive minister of the Colonial Church of Edina, Minnesota. Formerly he was executive director for Youth Leadership and was part of the National Training Staff for Young Life.*

BY DAVID C. McFADZEAN

The Glass Box

A ONE-ACT PLAY

Characters

Lisa, a teenage girl

Her Friend (male or female)

Her Parent (mother or father)

Her Teacher (male or female)

Note

This play is designed for minimal movement and may even be done as a reader's theater. The part of Lisa would be enhanced by movement, though she must sit the entire show.

Throughout the play, the characters all speak primarily to the audience. The others remain completely unaware of Lisa's presence, and somewhat unnoticing of one another's presence.

Another dimension may be added by having the Friend, Parent, and Teacher seated in the audience at the beginning and exit into the audience at the end.

The Glass Box

The stage is bare except for one stool center. The lights go out. In the darkness voices are heard calling out.

TEACHER: Elise? Elise!

FRIEND: Lisa!

PARENT: Leeeeeees! (Pronounced "lease")

(The voices continue in darkness. They build in intensity and begin to overlap until they are a confusion of sound. The voices stop abruptly. All is silent in the darkness for a few seconds. Then the lights come up on the stool center stage. LISA is sitting there alone. When lights come to full the voices are heard again.)

FRIEND: Lisa?

TEACHER: Elise! . . . Elise!

(LISA listens to the voices for a moment. She thinks for a moment.)

Illustration by Donna Nelson

LISA: No use calling back to them. I've tried. Doesn't work.

PARENT: Leeees!

LISA: My voice only bounces back at me. Off this.

(She puts her hands out in front of her against an invisible wall of glass.)

It's like a glass wall. You can't see it. No one can really. And only I can feel it because it can only be felt from the inside.

FRIEND: Lisa?

LISA: I think there might have been a time when I could have called back. Even stood up and pushed against the glass until the panes fell and were shattered all around me.

PARENT: Leeees!

LISA: But not now.

(Her hands search out the glass walls on all sides of her.)

Glass walls all around me now. Like a small glass box.

TEACHER: Elise!

FRIEND: Lisa?

LISA: It's here because of my problem. That's what everybody calls it. "My Problem." We're afraid to call it by its name. To make it real. That's one of the reasons this is here.

(She puts a hand on the wall.)

Because we're afraid. It wasn't built all at once and I don't know all the reasons it was built, but . . . I do know how all alone I feel in here. How helpless.

(The calling begins again. As they call, the TEACHER, FRIEND, and PARENT appear. They gather around the stool, but don't seem to notice LISA.)

FRIEND: It's terrible about Lisa being missing like this, isn't it? When her mother (father) called and told me, I felt awful.

LISA: One time, just after my problem began, I forget who it was, but somebody from my church youth group came up to the walls when you could still barely see through them.

FRIEND: I mean, it's not like we were best friends or anything like that, but I want to do whatever I can. That's what I told her mother (father).

LISA: He (she) looked through the walls and asked how I was feeling.

FRIEND: I don't really know her all that well. But . . . I do want to help.

LISA: I didn't say anything to him (her). I don't think he (she) really wanted to know how I was feeling. He (she) sort of smiled and told me that God was always with me.

FRIEND: I mean, even after her problem began I tried to be friendly with her and all that, but I . . . well, maybe I didn't really try all that hard. But I didn't know what to say to her. I guess I was embarrassed or something. Besides, I thought she wanted to be alone.

LISA: You know what?

FRIEND: I mean, what are you supposed to say anyway? "Don't worry, Lisa, everything's going to be all right." I knew that wasn't true.

LISA: When people who are standing right in front of you are having trouble seeing you, you begin to wonder if God really can.

FRIEND: I just wanted things to be all right for her, I guess.

TEACHER: It was her grades that first made me think something was wrong.

FRIEND: Is that so bad?

TEACHER: One week she's a B+ student and before you know it she's barely making C's.

LISA: They weren't always here, these glass walls.

TEACHER: It's not so unusual. Anything could have caused it. If I was going to list the reasons a student's grades fall off, we could be here all night.

LISA: At first I thought I was putting the walls up myself.

TEACHER: But it wasn't just the grades that tipped me off with Lisa. There were a lot of little things. And then yesterday. Yesterday I knew for certain something was bothering her.

LISA: A wall here and there made me feel a little more comfortable with people. But after a while you feel kind of closed in by everything.

TEACHER: She stayed after class. Just sat there at her desk for a moment like she was looking for something in her purse. But I knew better.

LISA: You begin to feel like you're not controlling the walls anymore.

TEACHER: I sat at my desk going over some papers and it flashed through my mind for just an instant that she wanted me to ask her if anything was wrong.

LISA: You feel so helpless.

TEACHER: Of course there was something wrong. Her grades were dropping; she was tired in class. You don't teach for 12 years without noticing the signs.

LISA: And then you realize something about the walls.

TEACHER: I let her sit there fumbling in her purse. It wasn't for very long, but in that moment I made the decision to ignore her. I just had too much on my mind that day.

LISA: You realize that all along you haven't been building the walls alone.

TEACHER: I felt bad about it, but you have to draw the line somewhere.

LISA: All of them were helping me to build them.

TEACHER: She came from a good family. I assumed they were helping work things out. After all, I have over a hundred different students every day.

PARENT: I knew she was hurting.

TEACHER: With a hundred different problems of their own.

PARENT: And I was hurting for her. I don't think she ever understood that.

TEACHER: You can't get involved in everything.

LISA: I almost forgot how funny the walls acted with some people.

PARENT: I think we had a good relationship before the problem.

LISA: When words could still pass through them, the walls would mysteriously change them. Actually change the words. Not with everybody. Mostly with people I was very close to.

PARENT: She got so defensive with me. I couldn't seem to break through to her and let her know how I felt.

LISA: I don't know if I can explain it, but I would be talking to someone and inside I would be thinking how lonely or painful I was feeling. But when my words went through the walls, they sounded so different.

PARENT: She thought I was ashamed of her or embarrassed to be her mother (father). I couldn't talk to her anymore.

LISA: It was like the walls would only let anger or bitterness pass through them.

PARENT: Everything ended up in an argument.

LISA: But they would never let my true feelings pass through.

PARENT: Something like this certainly makes you feel like a failure as a parent. I don't think Lisa ever heard how deeply I was feeling for her.

FRIEND: It's terrible about Lisa being missing like this, isn't it?

LISA: Just after the problem started I couldn't sleep very well, so I began staying up watching the late movie.

TEACHER: She was tired in class.

LISA: This one night I remember *The Invisible Man* was on. It's supposed to be sort of scary, I guess. But I only felt sorry for the man.

FRIEND: I mean, I tried to be friendly with her and all that.

LISA: And there was this scene in the movie where the man cried invisible tears.

PARENT: No. I'm sure she never heard me.

LISA: I knew, right then, exactly how sad he felt . . . being invisible.

(There is a pause. The FRIEND, PARENT, and TEACHER look around. They call quietly for Lisa as they slowly leave. Lisa is alone again. She looks out.)

LISA: Glass walls all around me now. Like a small, glass box. It wasn't built all at once, and I don't know all the reasons it was built, but . . . I do know how all alone I feel in here. How helpless.

(The lights fade in silence.)

□

David C. McFadzean *is director of the Theater Department at Judson College, Elgin, Illinois. Formerly, he was president and managing director of the Lamb's Players, a California-based Christian drama troupe. An accomplished playwright, David has had nearly half a dozen plays produced; one was optioned for an off-Broadway production in New York.*

Lord, Send a Fish and a Resurrection

Photography by Edward L. Lallow

WEEKEND RETREAT

BY DICK HARDEL

Aim

To help kids experience God's unfailing grace in their pits of despair.

Overview

Lord, Send a Fish and a Resurrection is a retreat designed to help participants deal with times when they are down and buried in the "pits" of despair. All of us find ourselves trapped in these depressions at different times in our lives.

This retreat deals with heavy events in the lives of the participants and focuses upon God's loving grace, which does not fail us. The presence of Christ opens windows of hope in our "pits" of despair and enlightens our lives. The message of love and forgiveness breaks through the walls of depression, anger, fear, and pain.

Note: This retreat is designed for youth groups that have been together for a while and have established community. I would not suggest using this retreat for a first-time experience and community builder.

You'll Need

- ☐ Bibles
- ☐ flashlight, penlight, or perhaps candle for each participant
- ☐ a cardboard box for each participant, one large enough to sit inside (a large appliance box)
- ☐ movie projector and screen
- ☐ newsprint and markers
- ☐ masking tape, transparent tape
- ☐ construction paper
- ☐ glue, scissors
- ☐ magazines
- ☐ Lord, Send a Fish and a Resurrection (activity piece BR1 from the back of this book)
- ☐ The Great Fish (activity piece BR2)
- ☐ The Shade Plant (activity piece BR3)
- ☐ Relationship Encounter (activity piece BR4)
- ☐ Films: *Everybody Rides the Carousel (Part II), Cipher in the Snow, Oh Happy Day*

SCHEDULE

Pre-retreat covenants

Friday

Leaving	Pre-retreat worship
8:00 p.m.	Arrive and get settled
8:30 p.m.	On the surface
9:30 p.m.	I know the feeling
10:00 p.m.	Break
10:15 p.m.	In the "pits"
11:15 p.m.	Film: *Everybody Rides the Carousel (Part II)*
11:45 p.m.	Pit stop #1: Psalm 18
Midnight	Rest well

Saturday

7:00 a.m.	Wake up and get ready
8:00 a.m.	Breakfast
9:00 a.m.	Pit stop #2: Psalm 69
9:15 a.m.	Bible study: Lord, Send a Fish and a Resurrection
10:20 a.m.	Break
10:30 a.m.	In the "pits" again
11:30 a.m.	Film: *Cipher in the Snow*
Noon	Lunch
1:00 p.m.	Relationship encounter
2:30 p.m.	Pit crews
5:00 p.m.	Windows of hope (events)
6:00 p.m.	Supper
7:00 p.m.	Pit stop #3: Psalm 116
7:15 p.m.	More windows of hope (people)
8:00 p.m.	Film: *Oh Happy Day*
8:30 p.m.	The door
9:00 p.m.	Preparation for people party
9:30 p.m.	People party
11:00 p.m.	Bonfire (with devotions)
11:30 p.m.	Party continues
11:50 p.m.	Pit stop #4: Psalm 73
Midnight	Rest Well

Sunday

7:00 a.m.	Wake up and get ready
8:00 a.m.	Breakfast
9:00 a.m.	Joy stop #1: Romans 10:5-17
9:10 a.m.	Sing from the "pits"
9:30 a.m.	Plan for worship
10:30 a.m.	Worship
11:30 a.m.	Clean up and pack up
Noon	Journey home

Pre-Retreat Events

Covenants are important for people who are sharing life together. At least one week before the retreat, participants should design their covenant for the weekend. Begin the covenant meeting by teaching the song, "Jonah" (below). Then give each participant a "Great Fish" (activity piece BR2 from the back of this book). Have each participant write:

- his or her name—on the fin of the fish.
- personal goals for this retreat—on one side of the fish. (Example: "Begin a close friendship with someone." Commit time and energy to these during the retreat.)
- how he or she needs the group to help accomplish the personal goals—on the other side of the fish.
- three things that he or she has to offer the group—somewhere else on the fish.

Have them share the things they wrote in groups of three or four.

Draw a huge fish on newsprint and tape it to a wall. Discuss how you will live with one another during this retreat: respect for others' rest, property; how we will deal with leadership; etc. Write on the huge fish the decisions of the group. Have participants tape their personal covenant fish onto the huge fish so their names are visible: This is their signature and means this is their covenant. Take the covenant fish to the retreat and put it up where it is visible.

Worship Before Leaving

Sing verse 1 of "Jonah" and the chorus. Have one person read Jonah 1:1-5 aloud (great by candlelight).

Sing verse 2 of "Jonah" and the chorus. Have another person read Luke 8:22-24.

Sing verse 9 of "Jonah" and the chorus. Read the following "Lord If" prayer.

Lord if
you can calm stormy
waters,
quiet the power of wind
with a word,
bring strength to people
weakened by fear,

go down to the depths
with Jonah and
love him even though he
tried to run away,
then you
can be with me when I am
down, deep,
and under and speak your
word
that lifts me from any crisis
and
restores me to the realm
of the living.

Have each participant write his or her own "Lord If" prayer. Then have participants speak the prayers aloud. Sing the last verse of "Jonah" with the chorus.

Jonah

This retreat theme song is sung to the traditional folk tune, "What Shall We Do with a Drunken Sailor?"

CHORUS: Lord, our God, have mercy on us; Lord, our God, have mercy on us; Lord, our God, have mercy on us; ear-lye in the morning.

VERSE 1: We sail a ship with a man named Jonah *(sing three times);* ear-lye in the morning.

VERSE 2: Fall on your knees, for the sea is raging. 3: Who is the guilty one among us? 4: Cast the lot, and the number's Jonah's. 5: Row, men, row to save this Jonah! 6: O Lord God, we've got to drown him. 7: Done, and the sea has ceased its raging. 8: Lord, send a fish and a resurrection. 9: What shall we do when the world is drowning? 10: Lord, send a fish and a resurrection.

Retreat Events

On the Surface

Ask participants to cut out a strip of construction paper. Have them use a color that describes a mood they are often in. On one side of the strip, they should list things about themselves known by others; on the other side, feelings few or no people are aware of. Have the kids form the strips into loops or necklaces and tape them. Be sure they keep the private feelings on the insides of their necklaces. Then, in groups of six to eight, have them share the outsides of their necklaces and inside feelings they are comfortable sharing.

Next, have each participant make a cross from construction paper. Loop one cross between two necklaces and tape it. Connect all the necklaces in this way to make a large paper chain.

I Know the Feeling

Have participants sit on the floor in a circle, facing in. Give each person a piece of paper with one feeling word (*mad, sad, glad, etc.*) printed boldly on it. With string or yarn, each person should hang the word from his or her neck so it can be clearly seen by all. Choose one person to be in the middle, and give him or her a "bopper" (newsprint rolled and taped, or a foam cushion; bop gently).

The game begins by the facilitator saying his or her feeling word and then saying someone else's word. The person in the middle quickly tries to find the person with the second feeling word and bop her on the head before she can say her feeling word and another person's word. If the person in the middle succeeds, they trade places so the bopped person becomes the new middle person.

In the Pits

Give each participant a large appliance box. (Or make tents with blankets and chairs, caves using newsprint and chairs, or four cardboard walls with the top covered with newsprint.) The boxes should be scattered throughout the room. Using markers, the participants should print their names boldly on the outside of their pits, along with crisis signs like: "Do Not Disturb, Crisis Going On," etc.

Next, have participants go inside their pits. Each person will need a flashlight and markers. Each person should draw on an inside wall symbols of events that bring him or her into the "pit," then spend five minutes thinking about those events.

On a second wall, participants should list all the people who bring them down into the pit, or people they have brought down into the pit. Then they are to spend at least five minutes thinking about those people. Bring them out of their pits and in groups of four have them share what it was like in their pits.

For "In the Pits Again," use a

third wall. Have participants write all the feelings they have about themselves when they are in the pit. Again, they should spend at least five minutes in meditation. Then on a fourth wall, they are to draw symbols of hope. After five minutes in silence, they are to come out and in groups of four share what it was like to be in the pit.

Pit Stops

The pit stops are Bible reading and meditation times. Each reading suggested shows God with a person in the pit. The participants should do the Bible readings in their pits using flashlights. An additional activity: have participants write a prayer after each reading and tape it to one of the walls of their pits.

Films

Many good films enable participants to see God's presence even when they are in the pits. The three suggested in the schedule are available from Mass Media Ministries, 2116 N. Charles St., Baltimore, MD 21218 (phone 301-727-3270). After each film, have small groups of about six share what they saw in the film.

Bible Study

This Bible study is designed for small groups of six to eight people. Distribute to each group a copy of the "Lord, Send a Fish and a Resurrection" Bible study sheet (activity piece BR1). Also give each person a pencil, Bible, three copies of "The Great Fish" (activity piece BR2), and one copy of "The Shade Plant" (activity piece BR3). An option would be to do the two parts of this study at different times.

Relationship Encounter

This encounter is done by pairs. Give each pair a copy of "Relationship Encounter" (activity piece BR4). Allow adequate time to work through the entire sheet.

Pit Crews

"Pit crews" is organized games and free time. Plan games in which the whole group must accomplish a task together.

Windows of Hope

Have participants make window collages of signs of hope, things that make light break through the walls of the pit for them. Have them put the windows on the outside of their pits.

The first time through, participants should think of *events* that gave them a lift out of the pit and cut out a different-shape window for each. For the second "Windows of Hope" time, participants cut out windows for each *person* who has brought the light of hope into their lives.

The Door

Have each participant draw a large door on his or her pit. On one side of the door, participants should list people who have shut them out, and also those whom they have shut out (use code names for any people in the group). On the other side, have them write prayers for the door people. Then have them cut out the doors. (You may want to use them for the bonfire and devotion later.)

People Party

Have colorful supplies so the encounter partners can make affirmation garments for one another for a "People Party." Participants make hats, ponchos, etc., to make their partners shine. For the party have music, good snack food, and a talent festival. Perhaps surprise the group with a performing group or funny movie.

Sunday Worship

Have small groups plan the worship service: Setting (banners, altar, balloons, etc.), Music, Praise time, Confession and forgiveness (you may want to use the bonfire again and burn the pits), Prayer and benediction. List the flow of the worship service so everyone can see it. Then have a great time in worship. □

Dr. Dick Hardel *is associate pastor, St. John's Lutheran Church, Winter Park, Florida. Dick has been involved in youth ministry since 1970 and each year designs scores of retreats.*

Activity Pieces A1 & A2

Crisis Checklist

Check any of the following crises you have experienced. Then try to find at least one person who has experienced each crisis you've checked.

CRISES	Initials of Friend Who Experienced Same Thing
☐ Someone close to me died.	________
☐ My dad lost his job.	________
☐ My mom lost her job.	________
☐ I lost my job.	________
☐ I had an operation.	________
☐ Someone in my family was sick in the hospital.	________
☐ I was in an accident.	________
☐ I lost something important.	________
☐ I got cut from a sports team once.	________
☐ I got sent to the principal's office.	________
☐ I got mugged or beaten.	________
☐ Someone close to me was mugged or beaten.	________
☐ I flunked a class.	________
☐ Something valuable of mine was stolen.	________

CRISES	Initials of Friend Who Experienced Same Thing
☐ Our house burned.	________
☐ Our house was broken into.	________
☐ My parents are divorced or separated.	________
☐ My best friend hurt me.	________
☐ I did something I wish I hadn't and felt guilty.	________
☐ I liked someone and that person didn't like me.	________
☐ My pet died.	________
☐ My brother or sister got in big trouble and everybody started treating me differently.	________
☐ My parents and I had a huge fight or argument.	________
☐ I hurt somebody really badly by something I did.	________
☐ I had to move when I didn't want to.	________
☐ Other (specify).	________

Sentence Starters

I feel I can handle my problems best when . . .

But, life gets rough when . . .

And I feel overwhelmed if . . .

When I read Genesis 3:19 that life is tough, I feel . . .

When James (1:2-4) says to consider it pure joy when trials hit me, I think . . .

Jesus' words (John 16:33) make me feel . . .

The Awareness Wheel

A helpful way to get to the center of a problem

To get to the heart of a difficult problem, it's a good idea to try to dissect all of the elements involved. Here is an exercise to give you practice in becoming more aware of what's going on inside you when you face a problem. Give this a try: Think of a problem you are facing right now. Write the concern in the hub (center) of the Wheel. Then write all the things that come to your mind about your problem in the appropriate spoke of the Awareness Wheel. If you have a hard time deciding which spoke to list your awareness under, that's okay. This will help you discover what parts of the Wheel you do not understand fully.

See how much information you can record about yourself and your problem. In which areas are you most aware? Least aware?

When you feel you understand your problem better and are able to describe it well, you can begin taking steps to solve it. One of those steps may be to talk to someone about it.

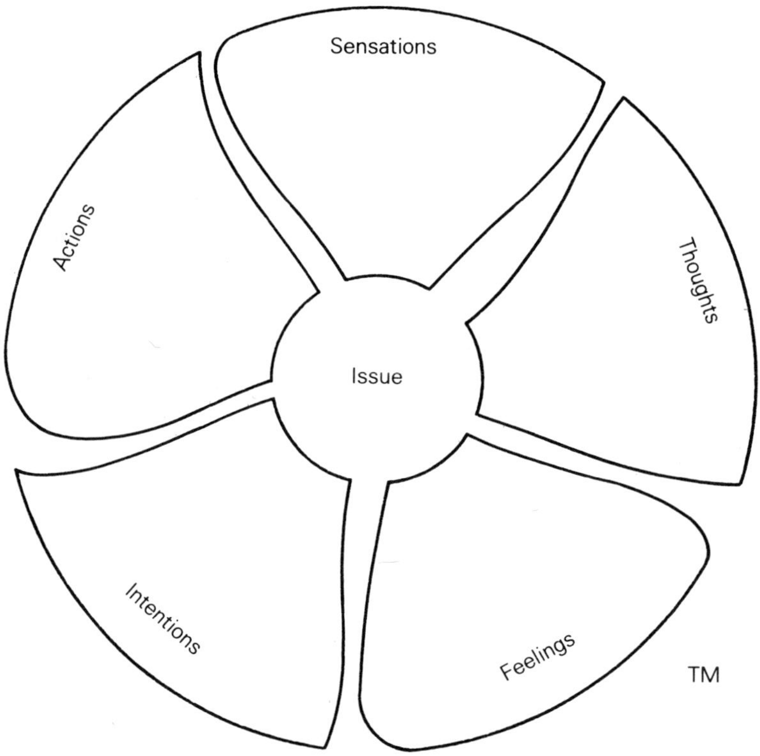

The "Awareness Wheel" is trademarked and was developed by Interpersonal Communications Programs, Inc., 715 Florida, Suite 209, Minneapolis, MN 55426. Authors Sherod Miller, Elam Nunnally, Daniel Wackman. Adapted by permission from *Talking Together.*

Activity Piece B2

Personal
INVENTORY

1. At times during this past year, I have felt really unhappy or "down." ☐ YES ☐ NO

2. I have a close friend who has been really unhappy or "down." ☐ YES ☐ NO

3. I know of someone who was feeling really sad or depressed but he/she is not a friend of mine. ☐ YES ☐ NO

4. I have been so unhappy that I have felt that life was not worth living. ☐ YES ☐ NO

5. What really depresses me is: ☐ YES ☐ NO

6. When I am down, the actions I take to change the situation are: ☐ YES ☐ NO

7. I have tried to hurt myself. ☐ YES ☐ NO

8. If I could talk to anyone about what makes me depressed, I'd talk to: ☐ YES ☐ NO

9. I have talked to someone about what gets me down. ☐ YES ☐ NO

☐ Male ☐ Female Grade:______

ACITVITY PIECE B2 by Paul Beggin, social worker and counselor, Mahtomedi High School, Mahtomedi, MN 55115

Activity Pieces C1 & C2

SUICIDE: MYTH VS. FACT

Find out the truth about suicide.

MYTH: People who repeatedly talk about killing themselves probably won't ever do it.
FACT: Most people who commit suicide give definite verbal and behavioral warnings of their intentions. When they threaten suicide, they need help. If others ignore their talk, suicidal persons may actually try to commit suicide, and perhaps succeed.

MYTH: If someone really wants to kill himself or herself, there is nothing anyone can do to stop him or her.
FACT: Most people who commit suicide want desperately to live. Even the most depressed person has mixed feelings about wanting to die, sometimes wavering until the last possible moment, and often giving obvious signals to others to help save them.

MYTH: Once a person is suicidal, he or she will always be suicidal.
FACT: The helplessness, depression, and suicidal thoughts last only for a limited period of time. If the suicidal or depressed person can find proper treatment during this temporary period, he or she can eventually be helped to a full, productive and enjoyable life.

MYTH: Someone who seems to improve after a suicide attempt probably won't do it again.
FACT: If the conditions that caused the first attempt are not identified and dealt with, the person may find it even easier a second time. Eighty percent of all suicide victims have made one or more previous attempts. Most repeated attempts happen about three months after what seems like "improvement."

MYTH: Suicide runs in the family.
FACT: Suicidal tendencies are not inherited. However, death in the family—whether natural, accidental, or suicidal—can lead to suicide if the resulting depression is not treated. Also, poor communication or lack of mutual respect within a family—especially between parents and children—can cause serious depression.

MYTH: Anybody who tries to kill himself or herself is basically crazy.
FACT: Although the suicidal person is extremely unhappy, he or she is not necessarily mentally ill. Most people who attempt suicide are depressed, or even clinically depressed, which means they can be treated medically or psychologically. Only a few attempters can be labeled psychotic or insane.

MYTH: Mentioning suicide in front of a depressed person will give him or her suicidal ideas.
FACT: Deeply depressed people already have those ideas. You don't put the thoughts in their minds. By bringing up the subject, you can help them talk about it.

MYTH: Suicide usually strikes only among the very rich or the very poor.
FACT: Rich and poor, male and female, young and old—every group is represented proportionately by suicide cases.

LOST & FOUND

Read the parables in Luke 15. Answer these questions as you think about what each parable means to you.

THE LOST SHEEP
(verses 1-7)

1. What might a lonely lost sheep feel when out there all alone?
2. When have you felt like the lost sheep?
3. Have you ever felt like one of the 99 sheep and watched someone wander away? Describe how you responded.
4. Describe which you would relate to best today: surrounded by one of the 99 (secure and friends), or the wandering sheep (all alone and isolated)?

THE LOST COIN
(verses 3-10)

1. What gives you a sense of your own worth?
2. What do you wish you had that would make you feel more valuable?
3. What makes you feel valuable to others?
4. Do you feel valuable to yourself? To others? To God?

THE LOST SON
(verses 11-33)

1. Which son do you identify with more? Why?
2. Describe what the prodigal son might have been thinking out there in the pigsty.
3. Can you identify with the father's feelings when his son returned?
4. What does God's forgiveness mean to you?

TOUGH STUFF

CASE STUDY CARDS

CASE STUDY 1

Your sister is always borrowing your stuff. She helps herself to your pens, pencils, clothes, and anything else she wants. Now she's taking over the computer you got for Christmas. The worst part is, your parents don't stop her. They say you should be willing to share with your little sister.

IS THIS SITUATION:

- ☐ A Piece of Cake!
- ☐ Tough Stuff
- ☐ Super Tough!

CASE STUDY 2

About two months ago, you took an after-school job at a fast-food joint because you need to save money for college. The only problem is that you never seem to have time to study. Today you receive your report card: mostly C's and D's.

IS THIS SITUATION:

- ☐ A Piece of Cake!
- ☐ Tough Stuff
- ☐ Super Tough!

CASE STUDY 3

One day right before school lets out, your counselor comes to your class and asks to see you. She sits you down in the faculty lounge and says, "I have bad news. Your mother just called. This morning your dad had a heart attack. He died about 20 minutes ago."

IS THIS SITUATION:

- ☐ A Piece of Cake!
- ☐ Tough Stuff
- ☐ Super Tough!

CASE STUDY 4

You have gone steady for two years, and now you and your fiancé have decided to set a wedding date. You're graduating soon and looking forward to the wedding. Then one Saturday night, your fiancé says, "You know, I've been putting off telling you this for weeks. I've met someone else."

IS THIS SITUATION:

- ☐ A Piece of Cake!
- ☐ Tough Stuff
- ☐ Super Tough!

CASE STUDY 5

Last night your sister, who's in tenth grade, told you she's pregnant.

IS THIS SITUATION:

- ☐ A Piece of Cake!
- ☐ Tough Stuff
- ☐ Super Tough!

CASE STUDY 6

All through high school, you've hung around with a great group of kids. There's only one problem: They are a year older than you. Now that they have graduated, you hardly ever see them and you don't have anyone to hang around with at school.

IS THIS SITUATION:

- ☐ A Piece of Cake!
- ☐ Tough Stuff
- ☐ Super Tough!

Activity Piece D2

CUE CARDS

The Pretenders

Skit Suggestions: Act out the complaint about the kitchen. Then pretend that no complaint has been made. You might change the subject, read the letter from the nursing home, etc. Try, in any way you can, to divert the conversation from the problem of the messy kitchen.

Don't Look at Me!

Skit Suggestions: Act out the complaint about the kitchen. Argue a bit, saying you couldn't have left the kitchen in a mess because you remember cleaning it up, etc. After the messenger leaves, start blaming everyone you can think of except yourselves.

The Avengers

Skit Suggestions: Act out the complaint about the kitchen. Act sullen and don't say anything to the messenger. You are angry. After he leaves, grumble for a while, getting progressively more furious. Finally you decide to get even with the church.

The Pity Party

Skit Suggestions: Act out the complaint about the kitchen. Then apologize and promise you'll never mess up the kitchen again. After the messenger leaves, start moaning and groaning about how you never do anything right, so why try to help people? Then end up by giving up trying.

The Quitters

Skit Suggestions: Act out the complaint about the kitchen. Then promise to keep the kitchen clean. But after the person leaves, start complaining about the adults in the church, the boring services, a youth group that gets only criticism, etc. Finally you all decide just to quit.

- 29 people under 18 will attempt suicide.
- 57 people under 18 will run away from home.
- 14 girls under 18 will give birth to illegitimate babies.
- 22 girls under 18 will receive an abortion.
- 685 people under 18 will take some form of narcotics—all regular drug abusers.
- 188 people under 18 will experience a serious drinking problem.
- 285 people under 18 will become victims of broken homes.
- 228 people under 18 will be beaten, molested, or otherwise abused by their parents.

Crisis Helper Guidelines

HOW TO HELP A FRIEND

1. Be available.
Be with your friend in crisis both in body and in heart. You may miss an opportunity to be an important helper if you let other things take priority over helping.

2. Expect that you can help.
Your relationship is what will allow you to be of significant help.

3. Try to have true empathy.
Empathy is "feeling your pain in my heart." Move alongside and have empathy, but don't say, "I understand," because you've never been in exactly the same situation.

4. Give a listening ear.
Sometimes the people who will become statistics are only looking for someone to listen. Often we are so preoccupied with ourselves that we fail to give them what they need most and costs least: our time and our attention.

5. Resist judging.
It doesn't help at all. Don't ever say someone's problem is stupid or use Scripture to pound him or her over the head.

6. Allow their feelings to flow.
God is not threatened by our words or our feelings. In the Psalms, David cried out to God with his frustrations. Let your friends be real with God so that they can work through what they feel.

7. Be a resource to resources.
The Bible says those who will be greatest are those who serve. Be willing to do things to help. Mow grass; take food; run errands. Move beyond the words. Prayer and the Bible need to be used here in the proper way. Praying with the friend in crisis communicates that we are limited but that we are in touch with the resources of Heaven. Sometimes a verse of Scripture is wonderful, but it must be given appropriately. It must let people know that God cares intimately about them. Crisis is opportunity to serve in the name of Jesus.

Activity Piece BR1

LORD Send a Fish and A Resurrection

A discovery Bible study on Jonah

Instructions

This Bible study is designed for small groups.

The facilitator of the small group will be the person who has the most experience in fishing. The facilitator's job is to make sure that everyone has the opportunity to respond to each part of the Bible study and to keep the study moving.

Part I

1. Complete one of the following and share with the group:
   a. When I think of fish stories I . . .
   b. The person in our family who has fished the most is . . .
   c. What one needs to be a great fishing person is . . .

2. Share your favorite fishing story (yours, your father's, grandmother's, etc.).

3. On the first "great fish," list as many things and events as you can that take you down and under (to the pits of despair). List the most difficult one on the belly of the fish. Share one of the events that takes you down with the others in the group.

4. On the second "great fish," list the times God said "Go!" and you tried to run and hide. Share with the group.

5. In a whisper voice, read together Jonah's prayer from deep inside the fish as written in Jonah 2:2-9.

6. Also on the second "great fish," write your prayer of confession from deep inside you. Pray the prayer (you may choose not to share this one).

7. On the third "great fish," write the following:
   a. a specific time God rescued you.
   b. a time God gave you a second chance.
   c. a time God turned a curse into a blessing (something meant to hurt you was turned into something to help you).
   Share with the group.

8. As a group, write two more verses to the song "Jonah" and sing them with the chorus.

Part II

9. Read chapter 4 of Jonah as a drama. One person be the narrator, another be Jonah, and a third be the Lord. Add movement and action to the reading.

10. On the "shade plant," write the following:
    a. a time something didn't turn out the way you thought it should.
    b. a time no matter what you did, you couldn't win.
    c. a time you were going to be angry no matter what.
    d. a worm that spoiled your shade (when things were going well and all of a sudden the bottom dropped out).
    Share with the group.

11. Rate your anger response and share with group.

    slow burner   sunburn   flaming nostrils
    forest fire   volcano   Nuke 'em

12. What calms you when you are angry? Share with the group.

13. Write two more verses to the song "Jonah" and sing with responses.

ACTIVITY PIECE BR1 by Dr. Dick Hardel

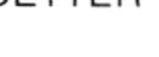

Activity Pieces BR2 & BR3

The Great Fish

The Shade Plant

Activity Piece BR4

A FACE-TO-FACE ENCOUNTER

DEVELOPING ONGOING RELATIONSHIPS

This encounter is a series of open-ended statements to help you examine your relationship with another person. The discussion is intended to be confidential.

All relationships periodically need renewal. This encounter provides an easy and nonthreatening structure to help you look at yourselves, who you are, and where you are going.

Tips for Good Communication

One important element in relationships is good communication. It is important that you:

1. Be open and accepting of your partner's responses.
2. Talk about your own feelings. Use "I" statements rather than "you" statements.
3. Feel free to skip any item.
4. Use this activity to share information, rather than to solve problems.
5. Be willing to take risks.

Open-ended Statements

1. One thing I really get excited about . . .
2. When I feel down, I . . .
3. I enjoy reading . . .
4. People I enjoy being around are . . .
5. I wish we had more time to talk about . . .
6. Something that worries me is . . .
7. My favorite TV program as a kid was . . .
8. My best subject in school . . .
9. My first pet was . . .
10. The chore I hate most is . . .
11. One way we are alike is . . .
12. One way we are different is . . .
13. One time I got in trouble in school was . . .
14. My favorite vacation was . . .
15. Right now I feel . . .
16. You are (could be) most helpful when . . .
17. One thing I regret having done is . . .
18. I really liked what you said about . . .
19. A habit of mine that bothers me most is . . .
20. My favorite room in the house is . . .
21. One thing I wanted to be when I grow up is . . .
22. I think your greatest strength is . . .
23. If I had $1,000 . . .
24. The things I most like to do (or would like to do) with you are . . .
25. I believe in and am committed to . . .